Homage Through Flowers

A Handbook

Sandra S. Hynson
and the
Washington Cathedral Altar Guild

Homage Through Flowers
A Handbook

© 1978 by Sandra S. Hynson
Library of Congress Catalogue No. 78-70750
Printed-designed by French/Bray Printing Co.
Glen Burnie, Md. 21061

for
Martha, Frank and Wayne
and Dick

Greetings:

   The Altar Guild is an essential part of the ministry of the Washington Cathedral as it is of every parish in the Church. Without the volunteer efforts of thousands of people around the world the sacramental life of the Church would be seriously hampered.

   I commend all of you who serve on altar guilds and pray for your continued commitment. I further hope that this book on church flower arranging will be of help to you in your work.

                        Faithfully,

                        + John T. Walker

                        John T. Walker
                        Bishop of Washington

PREFACE

For a number of years we have been besieged by flower committees asking the Washington Cathedral Altar Guild to publish a book on flower arranging for churches. There are many fine books on the art of flower arranging, but the specialized area of church flowers, unfortunately, has been neglected. The books we have recommended in the past now are out of print. No new ones have appeared to replace them. Therefore, we have gathered materials and pictures, helpful hints and warnings, anecdotes of joy and mishaps to compile a handbook for church flower arrangers. However, much of the material in this volume applies to all types of flower arranging. We hope this book will have universal appeal to all those who love working with flowers.

You will note the use of the pronoun "we" throughout. It is not the "royal we," but the combined "we" of the staff and some seventy volunteers who for many years have given thousands of hours of talent, time, ideas and love to beautify our National Cathedral.

PERSONAL and PRIVATE

Arranging flowers to the "Glory of God" is a privilege and a responsibility. To approach the task without joy and humility may rob the arranger of the spiritual satisfaction which comes from this particular offering of one's self. This often produces a less-than-best effort. A moment of quiet prayer at the altar rail, then, still kneeling, a fresh look at the cross and altar will help immeasurably in beginning the job with confident creativity. Such a prayer need not be formal or studied. It might be a simple and heartfelt, "Oh Lord, help me to return the beauty of nature which thou has given to beautify the altar for thy greater glory."

One Holy Saturday a relative novice of the flower committee was assigned a large pedestal arrangement. Feeling unsure of herself she stopped in Bethlehem Chapel to pray alone before presenting herself for work. She asked guidance that she might use the beautiful flowers to their best advantage for her Easter offering. In the first hour, after the completion of her mechanics and the establishment of her outline, she paused in uncertainty before placing her focal point of rubrum lilies. As she stood in thought two men approached and chatted quietly. Then she heard the one man say to the other, "Now, when she puts those lilies there and there, it will be smashing." We learned later that the man was a professional flower designer from New York. She did put "those lilies there and there," and produced not only a soul-satisfying, but a most beautiful offering for Easter Sunday. Her guidance was supplied.

For a more formal prayer we include Dean Francis B. Sayre's prayer for the Altar Guild of Washington Cathedral.

> We thank thee Lord for sacred places burnished by silent wings of holiness; for shrines consecrated by prayer, and lives suffused with thy quiet peace. Bless all who tend these sanctuaries, cleaning and adorning, that the offering of each one may reflect thy love and purity, and thy people rejoice in Christ Jesus lively in our midst. Amen.

TABLE OF CONTENTS

x

ACKNOWLEDGEMENTS

A project such as this never could have been completed without the encouragement, assistance and support of a great number of people. I wish I could name them all. However, my heartfelt and grateful thanks go to:

Altar guild women everywhere, especially *Phyllis Hayden; Mrs. Wayne Hood,* "our angel" whose gift was given in thanksgiving for the life of her mother, *Helen Hood Trane.*

My cathedral family, particularly all the members of the guild who read and criticized the rough drafts; *Jeanne Edwards,* a teacher of the Sekiso School and a student of the Ohara School of Ikebana, who contributed her vast knowledge to prepare Appendix 1 and to assist with Chapter III; *Bert Pence,* a local expert on foliage, who prepared Appendix 2 and assisted with Chapters IV and VIII; *Mary Miller,* my assistant, who kept the office operating while I wrote in the mountains and who typed and typed and typed; *Nancy Montgomery,* Washington Cathedral's Director of Communications and Editor of Cathedral Age who wrote the copy for the dust jacket; *Helen and Fred Fredlund* who corrected the final draft; *Bill Conkling* of French/Bray who has given so generously of his time and expertise in laying out the book.

To my family, especially *my parents* who laid the foundation at home and at Trinity Church, Baraboo, Wisconsin, where it all began; *Daughter Kit,* a paragon of selfless devotion, whose expertise in language and linguistics has made her an especially competent editor; But, most of all, to my beloved husband, *Dick,* who has personally tried each "step-by-step", taken nearly all the pictures and been at my side throughout.

Sandra Stekl Hynson

completed on my birthday
September 11, 1978
Washington, D.C.

I

ORGANIZATION

The Washington Cathedral Altar Guild is quite different in structure from a parish altar guild. Our seventy volunteers are divided into three committees which are responsible for the needlepoint, linen and silver and the flowers. Many of the duties, such as the laying out of vestments and the preparation of the eucharistic vessels, which are performed by the women of parish guilds, are handled by our cathedral verger and his staff. This not only gives us the necessary time to perform other duties required for the many and various activities scheduled at the National Cathedral, but it also allows each of us to concentrate on her own offering in the aim for that perfection worthy of our Lord.

The smallest committee is responsible for more than one thousand pieces of needlepoint for which the Washington Cathedral is justly famed. These women constantly inventory, rotate pieces for repair or re-upholstering, and choose designs and workers for occasional new pieces. As experts in this art form, they teach classes locally, lecture throughout the country, assist church women in setting up their own needlepoint projects, and answer a myriad of both telephone and mail inquiries.

The remainder of the volunteers are divided into four teams, each consisting of three-to-five linen and silver committee members and approximately twelve flower committee women. Each team is on duty for one week out of every month, beginning on a Friday and completing their service the following Thursday.

With conscientious love and attention the linen and silver committee maintains the sanctuaries of each of the nine altars with spotless fair linens and gleaming silver and brass. Twice a week the three-to-five duty members come in to dust, to polish and to burnish the crosses, candlesticks and alms basins, and to check the fair linens. The responsibility of the linen and silver committee is indeed a great one. The wonderful job they perform is most important for the maintenance of God's house. One never should under-emphasize the duties so painstakingly carried out over the year by each member of this committee, and for this they deserve high accolades. Since this book concerns itself primarily with the arranging of altar flowers, we will not delve further into the details of the various duties of the linen and silver committee. However, we do want to commend them for their devotion and careful tending of the cathedral sanctuaries.

The flower committee team captains report on Friday morning to help condition, sort and label the week's order of flowers. Sometimes arrangers will work on Friday afternoon when Saturday morning services or weddings are scheduled, but most of the arranging takes place on Saturday.

The captains instruct their team, having checked with the head of the altar guild on the containers to be used for each altar's selection of flowers, on the special preference of brides as to choice of design and on other out-of-the-ordinary requirements for the Sunday services.

Each succeeding day, Sunday through Thursday, a member or two of the team returns to water, refurbish, arrange flowers for special services and finally to take down the arrangements.

Though many churches assign their arrangers for a month's duty once or twice a year, we have found that a week's duty once a month provides better continuity and practice in the art of altar flower arranging. It is best to keep one's hand in throughout the year as this affords each member greater experience in handling flowers and greens of all seasons.

During Advent most of the altar arrangements consist of evergreens, although we may have occasional memorial or funeral flowers. Nearly all of the greens are cut from guild members' gardens or from the cathedral grounds. This represents a big saving for a flower budget. The restful and fragrant evergreens also suggest the semi-penitential season with its preparations for the joy of Christmas. Christmas will be discussed separately in Chapter X.

On the first Sunday after Epiphany we are likely to have a splash of spring flowers. Nothing revives the winter-weary spirits more than gay tulips, spicy stock, colorful iris and, for the small altars, delicate freesia and bright jonquils.

During Lent our altars are bare except for a funeral or a memorial service. This policy was begun as an observance of the penitential season. Even though Sunday is always a festival day, it seemed wasteful of flowers and manpower to arrange for seven altars to be decorated on Saturday and removed on Monday. We use these weeks to hold our flower arranging courses. They also give a respite for our guild members and time to plan, order and schedule for our glorious Easter festival. The altar flower arranging course is a prerequisite for new members of the guild. It also is available as a service to women of all denominations in the community.

On Palm Sunday morning the barren Lenten altars are decked with the traditional palm fronds to mark the beginning of Holy Week. As in the ancient church, we use a variety of materials to soften the stiff lines of the palm arrangements. Depending upon the date of Palm Sunday, and the advancement of the spring season, we may have pussy willows, forsythia, japonica, a variety of fruit tree branches or occasionally dogwood pruned from a guild member's tree. We also use the beautiful leaf of the elaeagnus commonly called Russian olive, the closest compromise to olive branches that Washington, D.C. can provide.

On Holy Saturday most of the guild members turn out en masse to decorate the entire cathedral in a matter of six or seven hours. Easter is covered in Chapter XI.

Following Easter, flowers are used weekly until the first Sunday in July. In July and August the stifling heat of Washington takes its toll on flowers so we again begin to use the native greens. Not only do the arrangements give the illusion of coolness, but arranged with pinholders and chicken wire they will last several weeks at a time when many of our guild members are away on vacation and the teams are cut in size. However, we still have special flower arrangements even during the hot summer months for funerals, memorials and weddings.

Formerly June was the traditional month of brides and many weddings were scheduled. Recently the trend is toward August and September weddings, perhaps to coincide with vacation schedules. The wedding policy of the Washington Cathedral is quite stringent. We discourage all brides who simply wish to use the Gothic beauty as a backdrop for a gorgeous wedding and we insist that local parish members use their own churches. However, Washington contains a transient population of non-parishioners. For these we gladly schedule some seventy weddings a year.

Each bride/bridegroom, or bride and her mother are interviewed. The bride may select the type of container used, the flowers and the colors she desires.

These are indicated by first and second choice on our "suggested flower and container" sheet. If two brides are being married on the same day in the same chapel they must agree on color or compromise on white. Since only one arrangement is done per week per chapel, wedding flowers are left as the bride's gift for the cathedral Sunday service. The bride's options are altar flowers or pedestal arrangements by the altar rail where the vows are exchanged. The flowers always are ordered and arranged by the cathedral altar guild. This is true also of funeral and memorial flowers to prevent variance in quality and quantity.

As the weather begins to cool during September, October and November we return to flowers.

Usually the first Saturday in October the cathedral Open House is scheduled with an invitation to the entire community to come and watch the cathedral family in action. During this day-long festival one can watch needlepoint demonstrations, bell ringing, stone carving, stained glass making, porch plays, chancel drama and flower arranging. The flowers on each altar are designed to represent certain festivals and special occasions such as Christmas, Easter, Thanksgiving, weddings, baptisms and saints' days. The arranging is staggered over a five-hour period so that interested flower arrangers may watch several types of arrangements being created. The guild members gladly answer questions, give advice and identify material for the public.

After the uplift of the Open House in October, the Altar Guild women return to a normal Sunday arranging schedule until Thanksgiving, the final festival of the Christian calendar, in late November. (See Chapter XII.)

Throughout the year team members are on call for duty with sometimes no more than forty-eight hours notice for funerals and memorials. As this is the only church chartered by Congress, and commonly referred to as the National Cathedral, memorial services are held here for American heroes, foreign dignitaries, members of Congress and other well-known people. We are responsible for the arranging of all the altar flowers, and the placing of memorial wreaths and baskets.

No matter how large or small, famous or parochial, wealthy or struggling the church may be, the altar guild of each church unites in spirit with all other altar guilds in the common purpose of administering, cleansing and decorating its own church for the greater glory of God.

We hope that our explanations will help church flower arrangers throughout the country to view their duties with fresh enthusiasm.

II

EQUIPMENT

Any job is done more efficiently with proper equipment. We are well stocked with the tools of our trade. Although some of the following items are used only once a year, others are required on a weekly basis.

A well-stocked arranging room contains

1. BASTER—a turkey baster is a most useful item to syphon water from filled containers
2. BLEACH—used as an additive to the water to prevent stagnation
3. BOXES—metal, varying in materials from brass and silver to aluminum and sheet metal. The sizes range from 7½″ x 3½″ x 2¼″ to 18″ x 11¾″ x 8″. The most commonly used measure 14″ x 3½″ x 3½″
4. BRICKS—for use in counterbalancing weight of frames, and as a base in dishpans to heighten oasis when creating a beehive (See Chapters V and VII.)
5. CEMETERY URNS—conical or cylindrical urns with heavy wire points for thrusting into grave sod are used to heighten arrangements or extend a number of stems
6. CLEANING MATERIALS—cleanser, scrub brushes, sponges, broom, dustpan and mop
7. COMPOTES—footed containers similar to a dining room table compote. These vary in materials from silver and brass to cement (bird baths), and in size from 2¾″ high and 4¾″ diameter to 11″ high and 14″ diameter

8. CONTAINERS—other than those spelled out individually, we use a selection of Ikebana containers, aluminum and plastic dish pans, urns, pots and vases in various locations throughout the church

9. CHICKEN WIRE—crumpled in containers in conjuction with pinholders it affords excellent stem support. (See Chapter VIII.) It also is used in frames for altar mechanics (Appendix 3)

10. CLIPPERS and KNIVES—garden clippers and rose knives for the cutting and trimming of stems and lower greenery; butcher knives for cutting oasis. We have kept our knives locked since choir boys were caught duelling!

11. FLORAL CLAY—a plasticene-type material to secure pinholders to containers, available in blocks and rolls. We do not recommend the tape variety as it is almost impossible to remove from the container

12. FLORAL PINS—U-shaped metal pins for securing fruit and dried materials to styrofoam forms

13. FLORAL TAPE—a green adhesive tape for mechanics of the beehive, and to adhere water picks to bamboo stakes, etc.

14. FLORAL WIRE—lengths of various weight wire for support of weak or wandering flower stems

15. FRAMES—plywood outlines for floral arrangement designs covered with chicken wire for support of greens and flowers (Appendix 3)

16. GREEN BAMBOO GARDEN STAKES—3 to 4 feet in length, purchased from a gardening center, and used for mechanics such as support and framework; also used with water picks taped to the end for extension of stem length (See Chapter VI.)

17. HOLDING CONTAINERS—any type of plastic bucket, vase, papier maché or ceramic container deep enough to hold the proper amount of water for conditioning prior to arranging. Must be kept immaculately clean

18. LEAD WEIGHTS—chunks, strips and puddles of lead used to counterbalance arrangements

19. NYLON STOCKINGS—pieces of discarded nylon stockings stretched over pinholders to prevent holders from becoming clogged with oasis or stems. After use simply lift stocking piece off before washing the pinholder

20. OASIS—foam bricks which absorb twenty times their weight in water; properties vary from instant, for quick absorption, standard which must soak longer but gives more support to larger stems, to spring oasis for fragile stems. Hint: Always dribble water over top of oasis to refresh arrangements. *Do not* water from side or bottom. If allowed to dry out after use, reconstitute by submerging in extremely hot water

21. PEDESTALS—any type of base, such as antique candlesticks, cut-off porch pillars, terra cotta chimney flues or square wooden pillars, which will hold a beehive for a free-standing arrangement

22. PINHOLDERS—needle holders of various sizes and shapes for mechanics in supporting stems

23. PLASTICS—sheets to protect altar while arranging; also used under containers which might mar the retable; pint and quart size freezer bags for bagging poinsettia plants and constructing garlands (See Chapter X and XI.)

24. PLASTIC SPRAY—a material such as Floralife Superior Surface Sealer for use on dried materials or certain shattering materials. *Never* use on outside of fruit

25. PLIERS—to open wires of florist greens or to bend chicken wire

26. PRUNING SHEARS—heavy-duty long-handled pruners for cutting heavy branches

27. SHELLAC and BRUSHES—to preserve fruits and vegetables for arrangements

28. SAUCERS—terra cotta and ceramic, varying in diameter from 8 to 16 inches as a basis for beehive construction in free-standing arrangements

29. STYROFOAM—sheets, cones and cylinders to support fruit, vegetables, etc. for festival arrangements

30. TOWELS—huck or terry cloth for drying containers and as a protection for fair linen when watering floral arrangements

31. TRASH CAN—preferably covered

32. TWISTEMS or POLYTWIST—rolls of green paper or plastic-covered wire used in mechanics of bamboo framework; to hold stems and branches in position; to fasten bagged poinsettia plants to frames; etc.

33. VASES—brass, silver and gold; some narrow-necked, some flared and varying in height from 4 to 20½ inches

34. VEGETABLE PEELER—to remove bark and fibrous stem layers
35. WATERING CANS—a long-spouted one for ease in reaching retable containers and two gallon size for transporting water in quantity
36. WATER PICKS—vials of various sizes with rubber snap-on caps with a hole in the center for the flower stem; used in case of a broken stem, or to elongate a stem. Substitute: a test tube with a balloon for the cap
37. WIRE CUTTERS—for cutting floral and chicken wire. *Never* use floral clippers for this purpose
38. WIRE HANGING BASKETS—from 8 to 14 inches in diameter for the construction of beehives in vases and free-standing arrangements (See Chapters V and VII.)
39. WOODEN FLORAL PICKS—available in a variety of sizes with wire attached to wrap around grapes, dried material, etc. when placing on styrofoam forms for festival arrangements
40. YARDSTICK—a necessity item for measuring the limits of an arrangement

III

PRESERVATION of CUT FLOWERS and FOLIAGE

The care and preservation of cut flowers and foliage is as important a study as the mechanics and placement of the flowers themselves. Not only is it economical to have flowers last as long as possible, but in church arrangements it is imperative that the arrangements retain their freshness while on display. Nothing is more disheartening than the sight of dead flowers on an altar.

Each Friday morning when a new team takes over, the weekend order of flowers is delivered. The flowers and greens are cut, stripped, sorted and placed in water for hardening. The holding containers are an assortment of WELL SCRUBBED florist buckets for the long-stemmed materials, and a wide variety of vases and papier maché containers for the shorter stemmed flowers and greens.

None of us likes to bathe in ice cold water, and neither do flowers. If the containers have not been filled a day ahead to allow the water to reach room temperature, we add enough hot water to make the water tepid. For Gerbera daisies, too-tight gladioli and certain other flowers, the temperature is raised to "baby formula" degree.

BASIC WATER METHOD

The two greatest villains causing flower loss are bacteria and air because they clog the stems and prevent water consumption. The material must be stripped of all leaves which would be below the water level, as submerged leaves decay causing bacterial growth. A dirty bucket retains the bacterial residue from prior standing water, therefore we scrub each container with cleanser and brush and thoroughly rinse immediately after finishing every arrangement. When a flower stem is cut air seeps into the lower stem and blocks the continuous flow of moisture to the blossom. If this can be prevented the flower will live much longer. The ideal way to avoid air in the lower stem is to cut the stem at a greater than 45° angle while it is under the water. When this is done the container to be used should be at hand so that a quick transfer can be made. This basic water method is recommended for all cut material.

Some stems, such as chrysanthemums and hydrangeas, should have their stems crushed rather than cut. Branches of greens will absorb more water if the stem is split into four parts and the bark pared off with a vegetable peeler three inches above the cut end. All of these procedures will increase the area of water absorption.

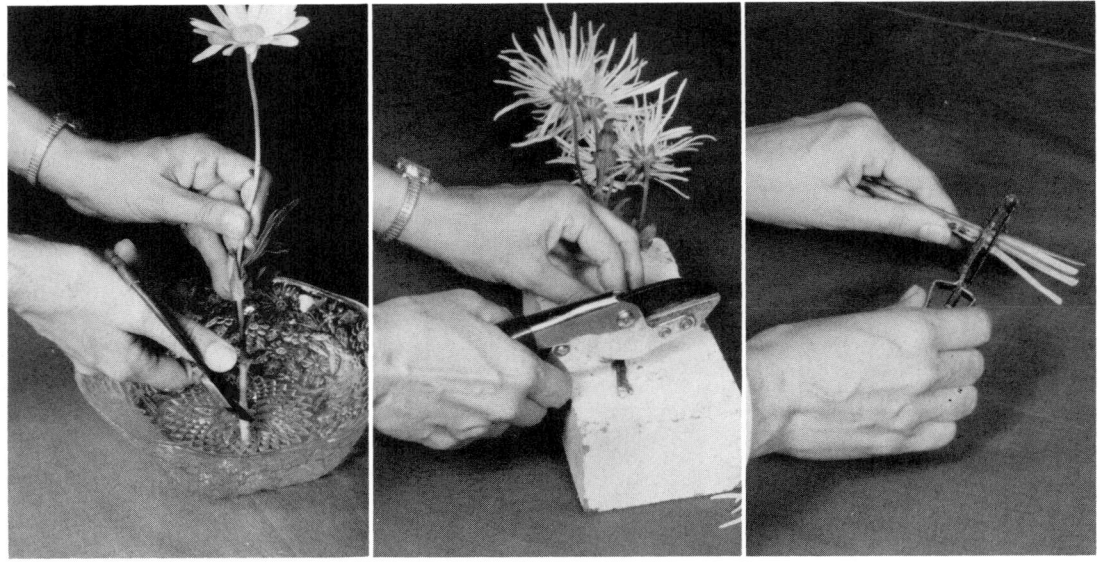

Flower arrangers also are grateful to the Japanese for four other methods of conditioning which we have borrowed. They are:

VINEGAR METHOD

This method is commonly used and is excellent for almost all materials. Experiment and learn to use it. The proportions are one part vinegar to three or four parts water. It is one of the fastest, easiest and least expensive of the various methods. It is especially recommended for green maple, reeds, pampas grass, other grasses and bamboo. If the material is young and fragile go through the usual water treatment, place it in the vinegar solution, then cut and leave for a minute. If the material is thick, woody and not so delicate use the vinegar water in place of fresh water. Leave the material in the solution overnight. Some flower masters use a weak solution of one part vinegar to four parts water in the vase after the flowers have been arranged.

FIRE METHOD

The stems of plants which exude a milky substance when cut, such as poinsettia, herbaceous peony and elaeagnus, should be held over an open flame. Wrap the flowers or greens with paper to protect them before this treatment. Keep the stem over the fire until the end is reddened, then immediately immerse in deep water. Be careful that the charred portion is not broken.

BOILING WATER METHOD

For a large bouquet the boiling water method is more suitable. Wrap the flowers with paper so that the steam will not hurt them, leaving only the ends of the stems exposed. Place the stems (about one-quarter inch) into boiling water—one minute for soft stems; three minutes for chrysanthemums; five for branches; then put the bouquet into deep cool water. This method is particularly effective for flowers such as roses, chrysanthemums, daisies, hydrangeas and dahlias, the stems of which are firm on the outside, but soft within. Boiling water forces air within the stems to expand slightly and escape. Do not be concerned if the submerged parts of the stems lose color. They will become sturdy once again when immediately put into cold water because the stems will contract, thus bringing up fresh water. *THE MOST IMPORTANT THING IS THE QUICK TRANSFER FROM HOT TO COLD WATER.*

CHEMICAL METHOD

When using any chemical the general procedure is: First cut the stem while it is immersed in water, then dry the stem, and finally apply the chemical.

11

The most commonly used chemicals are peppermint oil, alcohol (whiskey, vodka, etc.) and hydrochloric acid. The latter is not recommended because extreme care must be exercised in its use. The alcohol method is commonly used and is an excellent aid. Use only grain alcohol, not rubbing alcohol. After the usual basic water treatment, and before placing in the container, dip the stem into one-half inch of alcohol for a second or two and place in water immediately.

After being treated by any one of these methods of flower preservation, flowers *ALWAYS SHOULD BE PUT INTO DEEP WATER AND PLACED IN A DARK CORNER PROTECTED FROM SUNSHINE AND WIND.* Whenever possible they should be left overnight.

We cannot stress enough the need for (1) immaculately clean containers, (2) no submerged greenery and (3) proper clipping of stems.

If one or more of the flowers droops, before discarding it try reclipping it under water and placing it in deep, quite warm water with the head supported against the lip of the container. This emergency treatment often will revive a much-needed flower.

Water additives can be very helpful in prolonging the life of flowers. A substance, such as Floralife, added to the holding or conditioning water may produce dramatic results. However, when the flowers are arranged in brass or silver altar containers *plain water* must be used as certain additives are corrosive. In the case of greens, marigolds, zinnias and particularly baby's breath, the addition of one tablespoon of bleach per gallon of water will retard bacterial growth and help prevent offensive water odors. This is not destructive to the container.

Many flowers last longer if most of their natural green is removed. A good rule of thumb is "when in doubt remove the green!" Common sense tells us that a cut stem can supply only so much water, and since our prime concern is the blossom, feed it, not the leaves. Other greens can be added for stem cover. In the case of roses, Marguerite daisies, calendulas and lilacs the removal of the green is a necessity. One leaves on their lovely natural green only to return to church the next morning to find the flower heads wilted or drooping.

In the conditioning of some flowers, such as snapdragons and spider chrysanthemums, a fair depth of water is needed. Roses and Gerbera daisies should be placed up to their necks in water. Most flowers will benefit from a gentle tepid misting to compensate for evaporation. When gladioli arrive so freshly cut as to be barely showing color, their opening can be encouraged by first placing the stalks in quite warm water, then peeling back the protective green sheath from the buds, and finally misting with warm water. We'll never forget one Easter when twenty bunches of gladioli arrived looking like sticks on Good Friday. They couldn't possibly show by Easter, so two devoted women sat for three hours and peeled the buds of two hundred gladioli.

Greens suffer an almost greater loss by respiration than by stem water loss. A good soaking of the leaves themselves will greatly retard leaf dry-out. This is particularly true of fern. Longer branches can be heavily misted when submersion is impossible.

Materials selected from the garden should be cut in the cool of the day, the stems clipped under water, as previously explained, and then placed in water to a depth equal to at least one third the length of the stem. Sprinkle or spray the leaves with water. The technique of cutting stems while immersed in water should be applied immediately after taking them from the garden, and then repeated at the time of doing the arrangement. Once the correct length has been determined, cut the stem under water just before placing the flower in the container. Before you begin your arrangement place a small bowl of water at hand for this purpose. When making the arrangement care also should be exercised to ensure that the immersed part of the stem is completely defoliated.

All plants should be in a healthy state before any of the foregoing treatments are applied. Most plants can be revitalized by the method already mentioned of cutting the stems while immersed in water, sprinkling the leaves, and then standing them in fairly deep water. A second method of plant restoration is to sprinkle the underside of the leaves with water and wrap them in damp newspaper. In either case the plants then should be kept for several hours in a cool dark place before beginning the arrangement. This procedure is particularly effective for plants which have been transported over a long period of time.

Flowers Requiring Special Treatment:

Tulips

When tulips are brought to the flower arranging room the stems are clipped, lower green removed and placed in a tall, narrow container to keep the stems from curving. If no tall container is available the stems can be wrapped in newspaper to keep them straight. Tulips are stored in a dark, cool cupboard overnight to retard opening and stem distortion. As the tulips are arranged two steps are essential: (1) A tiny slit or hole is made with the tip of a rose knife or pin in the stem at the base of the flower head. This permits air to escape from the stem and promotes water consumption. (2) Every flower is wired. Tulips are notorious for "wandering," and must be wired to prevent them from turning to face a light source. Tulip wiring is a precise chore and must be done carefully as the stems are very brittle.

Two methods which we do NOT use on tulips are inserting the wire into the base of the tulip and twisting the wire down the length of the stem, or inserting the wire horizontally through the stem, bending the end down one-quarter inch and then wrapping the wire down the stem. As tulips continue to grow after cutting neither of these methods is satisfactory. In the first case the tulip head grows out of the wire and wanders where it pleases; in the second the stem is slit as it continues to grow past the horizontal wire hook. These two methods we reserve for roses, carnations, majestic daisies or any of the heavy-headed flowers to add support to the stems. There are two other

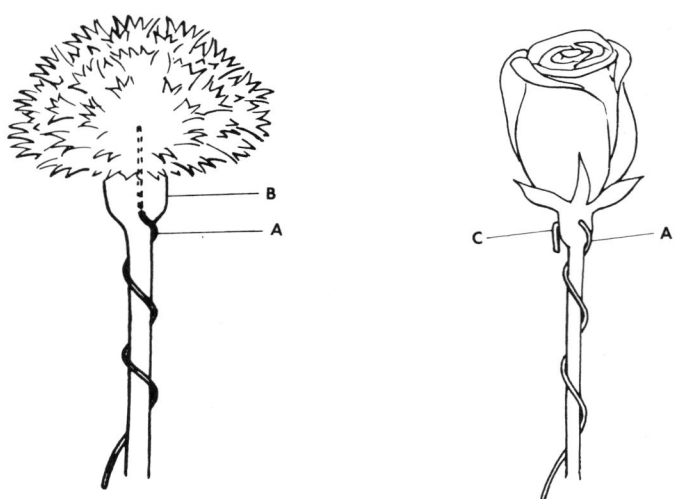

The two methods we use for wiring carnations, roses, majestic daisies or other heavy-headed flowers are: the wire (A) is inserted into the pedical (B) the longer end is then wrapped down the stem or the wire (A) is pushed through the pedical and bent over (C) before wrapping the longer end around the stem.

methods which we employ and have found satisfactory solutions to the wandering tulip dilemma. One is to fashion a curved wire cradle to fit snugly to the pedical (the enlarged green top of stem at the base of the petals). The wire then is wrapped carefully around the stem, leaving some play in the wire so that as the tulip grows it will not cramp the stem. The other method is used by some Japanese schools of arranging which permit wiring. Carefully open the blossom and insert the wire through it and down into the stem. Leave a length of wire in the blossom as long as the stamin and pistil so the flower cannot grow out of it. Then close the petals and pinch the stem very gently just under the blossom. This method will retard the opening of the tulip and will, in fact, prevent it from opening fully. Number nineteen wire should be used in either case.

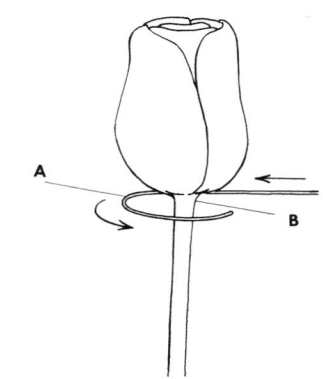

To wire tulips curve the wire (A) carefully around the pedical (B) to form a cradle (C) before loosely wrapping (D) the longer end around the stem.

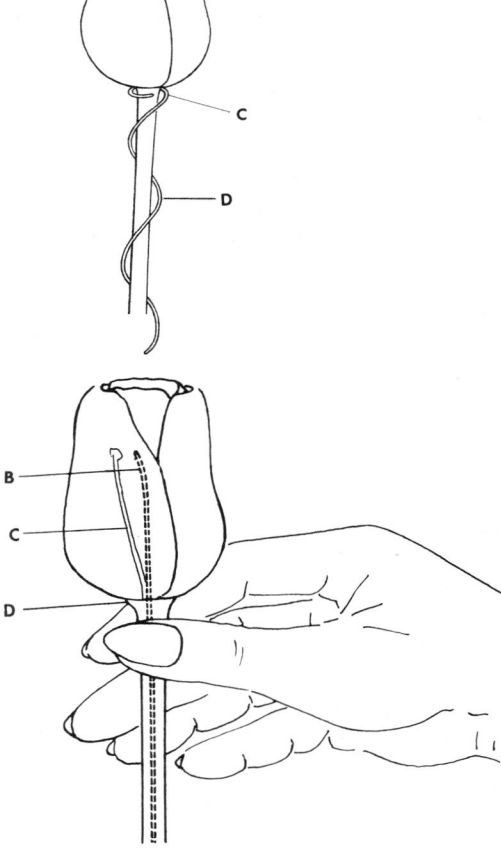

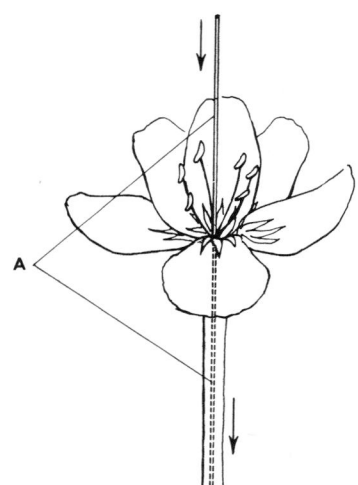

To use the Japanese method of wiring tulips, gently open the petals and insert the wire (A) through the blossom into the stem. The top length of the wire (B) must be as long as the stamen (C). When the petals have been reclosed the pedical (D) is pinched to prevent opening.

15

Anthurium

Although anthurium are expensive to purchase, this exotic Hawaiian flower may prove to be economical for massed color and longevity. Properly cared for anthurium can last a month. When received they should be totally submerged in tepid water for an hour. Be very careful not to touch the flower as fingers will produce a brown spot and begin the decay of the blossom. After submersion remove the bottom inch of the stem, preferably under water, and condition in tepid water for at least four hours before arranging. A regular misting with warm water will extend their lives.

Stock

The spicy fragrance of stock always is a welcome harbinger of spring. Being a member of the broccolli family, we condition stock as one would prepare the vegetable. To increase water absorption a vegetable peeler is used to remove two or three inches of the tough outer fibrous stalk from the cut end. The natural green is almost totally removed.

Lilies

Lilies present a special problem for altar use. Before they are arranged all pollen laden anthers must be removed. Pollen stains the fair linen and is impossible to remove without harmful over bleaching. As future buds open they should be watched and the anthers carefully removed.

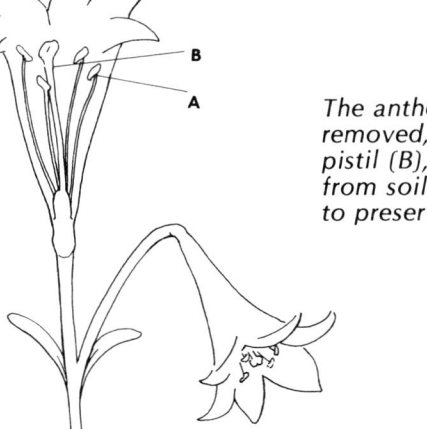

The anthers of lilies (A) are removed, without touching the pistil (B), to prevent their pollen from soiling the fair linen and to preserve the flowers.

Iris and Acacia

Garden iris "bleeds," and acacia "shatters" so they require careful attention. The purple stain known as "iris ink" discharged from shrivelled iris blossoms is impossible to bleach out without danger to the linen. To prevent such stains the wilted flower must be removed immediately as the next bud opens. Acacia adds a bright touch of yellow and a graceful shape to a bouquet, but its tendency to shatter its fine yellow dust on the fair linens or retable makes it a hazard. To prevent this from happening the flower should be sprayed before arranging with hair spray or a product such as Floralife's Superior Sealer.

Economics

Probably the most used altar flowers are gladioli and chrysanthemums. The reasons are obvious — they are relatively inexpensive for showy mileage, dependably long lasting and available throughout most of the year. Carnations also fall into the available category, though not nearly as long-lived as chrysanthemums. Chrysanthemums can be used a second Sunday if they are removed from the oasis or arranging material, reclipped, placed in clean water and stored in a cool, moist place.

The choice of the kinds of materials and the quantity used is dependent upon the flower guild's budget. However, proper conditioning and care should be given to all flowers and greens whether garnered from the roadside or purchased from a florist.

IV

THE PRINCIPLES OF ARRANGING

Flower arranging need not be a mystery. As one of our best flower arrangers said, "It's a matter of a good eye and common sense," and to go one step further, practice and constant self-critical judgment.

There are a few basic rules which make handling flowers for an altar different from other flower arranging. In the following eight premises you will find these rules, plus basic information which will assist you in decorating other areas of your chuch or synagogue, and your homes as well.

Let us begin with the size. The first premise is that flowers are placed upon the retable (or altar area) to *enhance the cross.* If they overpower or intrude upon the prominence of the cross they are improperly self-important. Hence, a good rule of thumb for an average Sunday service is that the height of the arrangement does not exceed the height measurement of the cross arm of the cross. To ensure the proper height and proportions of your arrangements, the measurements of the total height of the cross and the height of the cross arm of each cross on the altars in your church should be displayed prominently in the sacristy as a guide for reference. For striking variations on festival occasions the cross may be incorporated into the flowers so that the greens and/or flowers frame it. On these occasions the arrangement does exceed the height of the cross, but done with care this kind of design emphasizes, first and foremost, the importance of the cross.

What are the measurements of your cross? Chapel cross? What are the proportions of the altar to the reredos and the cross to the altar? Undoubtedly you already have ascertained that carnations will scale to the altar and perhaps miniature carnations to the chapel altar. In our case football chrysanthemums used at the high altar take on the scale of carnations used at a more normal size altar. This brings us up to premise number two.

a pair of gold vases for the High Altar: beehive mechanics: greens, salal: flowers, red gladioli and carnations, orange gladioli, yellow gladioli

brass vase arrangements for Bethlehem Chapel: greens, Baker fern and salal: flowers, white gladioli and Fuji pompom chrysanthemums, yellow Marguerite daisies

box arrangements for the High Altar: greens, cherry laurel: flowers, white gladioli, Fuji chrysan-
themums and carnations

one of a pair of compotes for St. Mary's Chapel: greens, Baker fern: flowers, Golden Wave roses and gypsophilia

one of a pair of box arrangements for War Memorial Chapel: greens, cherry laurel: flowers, red gladioli and carnations.

*box arrangements in St. John's Chapel to accent frontal: greens, ti leaves: flowers, Friendship
and Spic and Span gladioli, tangerine carnations, Mid-Century lilies
photo: Barrett*

one of a pair of pewter pedestal arrangements for the High Altar sanctuary: greens, salal and aucuba: flowers, white gladioli and starburst chrysanthemums, Bridal pink roses
photo: Wensink

a pair of converted wrought iron candlestick pedestals: greens, boxwood and Baker fern:
flowers, red and pink carnations, pink miniature carnations

font pedestal (Dun Font, Bethlehem Chapel): greens, salal: flowers, yellow and bronze snap-dragons, Golden Wave and Sonia roses, apricot Peter John chrysanthemums

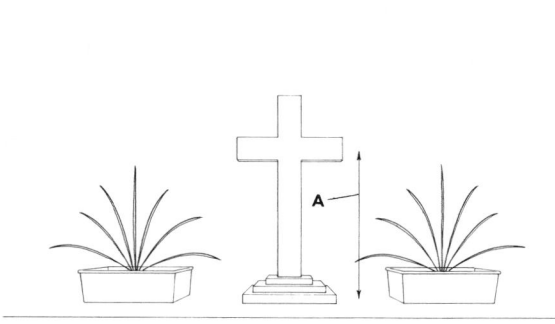

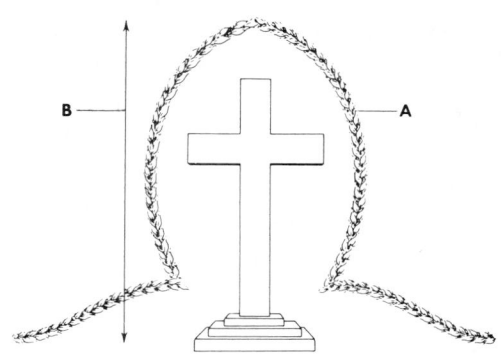

For an average Sunday the height of the flowers should not exceed the measurement of the cross arms of the cross (A).

On festival occasions the flowers and/or greens may frame the cross with an arrangement such as this vesica design (A) which exceeds the height of the cross (B).

The person in the last pew deserves to see and appreciate the beauty of nature as much as one in the first pew, so *scale and mass must always have this worshipper in mind.* Queen Anne's lace will carry singly in a small chapel, but will fade from view unless grouped en masse in a larger church. Unless specific colors are placed together, a mixed color bouquet will become "oatmeal" to someone in the far seat. When an arrangement is finished and put in place *never fail* to view it from the back of the church before making final adjustments.

The third premise concerns the *positioning of the worshippers.* In many churches the sanctuary is several steps *above* the nave, the altar several steps *above* that level and the retable *above* the altar. One should think in terms of a seated or kneeling congregation. The flowers and cross will be viewed from a number of inches below. Hence, in creating an arrangement, preferably on a counter at least forty inches high, one should bend down to view it from the worshipppers' angle many times during arranging. Begin by placing your spike material, i.e. snapdragons, gladioli, stock, etc., at an angle toward the front. Viewed from below these will appear straight. Then bring the round materials, such as chrysanthemums, carnations, etc. out in the front to create a bosomy effect. Vary this material in and out to ensure a dimension of depth.

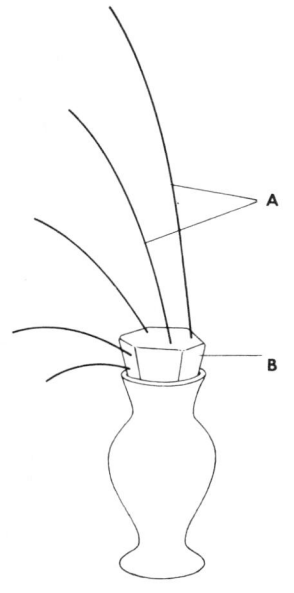

The side view of a vase shows the spike materials (A) placed into the oasis (B) at the forward angle. These will appear straight from the congregation and give better depth and dimension to the arrangement

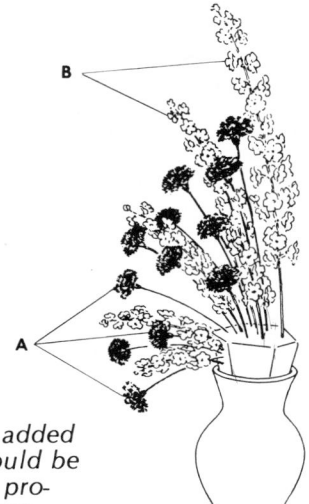

When the rounds (A) are added to the spikes (B) they should be placed at varying depths protruding forward in a bosomy fashion to create added depth and dimension.

When placing the flowers, the *direction of stems* is probably the most difficult for a novice to master. This is premise number four. One must decide where the root ball of an arrangement is located. This root ball is an imaginary clump or bulb in the focal point of the arrangement from which all stems must emanate as if it all were a living plant. If the root ball is located in the center of the box, the stems would be arranged as shown in Diagram 9. However, if the root ball is at one end (from candles to cross) or the other end (from cross outward) the root ball would be as shown in Diagram 10. This principle holds true in every type of arrangement, no matter what the container.

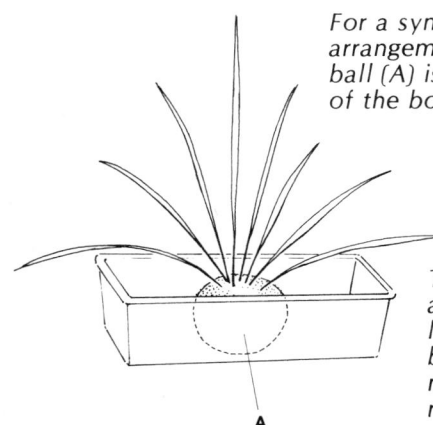

For a symetrical triangular box arrangement the imaginary root-ball (A) is located in the center of the box.

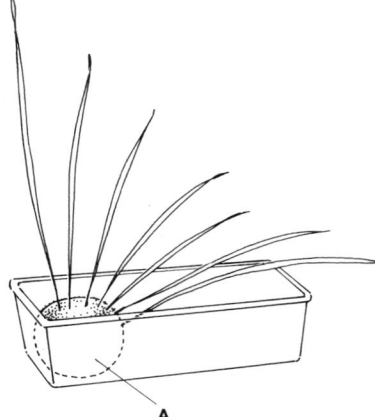

The rootball (A) for a right angled triangular arrangement is located at the left corner of the box. The other box of the mirror-image pair will have its rootball on the right.

The fifth premise is a basic flower arrangers' axiom, but applies all the more in altar arranging viewed from afar. *Keep the weight low!* Whether the mass be in weight of flowers or in their color, the heaviest must be kept close to the rim, or lip, of the container. A top-heavy arrangement will give the worshippers the uneasy feeling that at any moment the arrangement may come toppling down. By keeping heavy flowers low, and establishing a good bottom line of green, the flowers will appear firmly joined to the container, and assume a pleasing weight and stability.

This bottom line brings to mind the sixth premise of *the staggered line*. Nowhere in an arrangement should the material ever create a straight line, but this is particularly important at the bottom where the lower flowers must be uneven in position and depth.

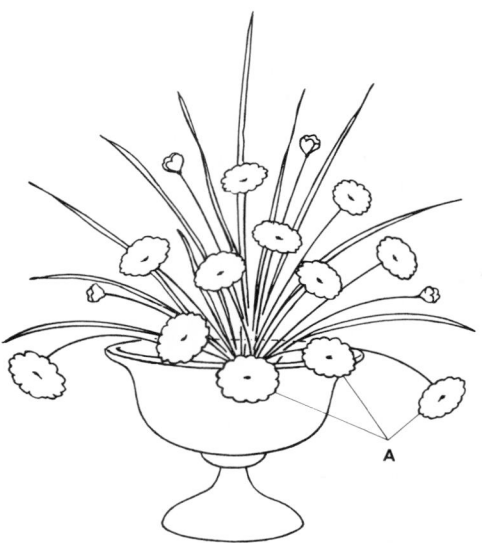

The round type material should never create a straight line. This is most important with the bottom line of the arrangement (A).

Good mechanics take a few more minutes before arranging begins, but the time is well spent. If mechanics are haphazard, disasters can result in more time wasted repairing, or redoing, a crumbled or toppled arrangement, so keep premise number seven in mind.

Matching a pair of altar arrangements is premise number eight. Remember that the pair must be constructed in a mirror image, as nearly alike as possible, with the only variance being Mother Nature herself. By mirror image we mean each arrangement is the exact opposite of the other. It makes no difference to the viewer if the two arrangements are symetrical, but it is essential if the designs are asymetrical. Often beginners will create identical asymetrical pairs which when put in place flow in the same direction instead of opposing each other. The working of a matched pair will be discussed in each of the succeeding chapters on containers.

With these eight principles well in mind, much of the mystery of flower arranging is eliminated.

Besides the basic premises, an understanding and appreciation of design, space, line, texture and color give additional confidence to create better and more effective arrangements.

Fundamentally, design is the planned use of space. Of primary importance are the spatial relationships which must be considered when plant material and containers are selected for altar arrangements. Every leaf, every blossom, every branch has line, texture and color and each occupies space in varying degrees.

Space is a design tool and an important unit within the arrangement which should be in harmony with its surroundings. Space occurs in Nature in many different ways, from the lacy spaces created by dainty flowers and tree foliage to the vertical space of tree trunks in a grove.

Line may be straight, curved or angular. It defines shape and creates the skeleton of composition. A vertical line indicates dignity, nobility, vigor and strength; the horizontal expresses a feeling of calm, solemnity and security; the diagonal line, like lightening, suggests dynamic action, danger and speed, while the curved shapes express softness and grace.

Texture describes surface structure. The smooth reflects light, as in the silky down of the milkweed or the waxy anthurium, whereas the rough is dull and absorbs light, like teasel or zinnias.

Of all the elements of design, color has the strongest emotional appeal. The importance of this emotional impact determined long ago the colors which traditionally express the feelings we experience during the various phases of the church year and our lives. The dramatic combination of red and green thrills us at Christmas, fresh, gay pastels warm our hearts in the great expectation of spring, and white connotes the sense of youth, purity and beautiful solemnity of a wedding. Dramatically different feelings may be achieved depending upon the mass of color and the balance between light and dark.

Before beginning any placement of materials decide upon the design and effect, bearing in mind the flowers to be used and their appropriateness for the occasion. Arrangers vary in their approach to the actual arranging of their flowers. Some start with flowers and fill with greens, while others establish their green background first, add the flowers, then cover mechanics and stems with remaining greens. Either produces lovely results. Several variables must be kept in mind, however. For example, if the reredos is stone or marble of a light color and white flowers are being used, only a solid green background will frame the flowers for visibility. On the other hand, if the reredos is dark wood, or the dossal is a dark color, the white flowers will stand on their own with only a lacy fill of greens. Since most of our reredos in the cathedral are carved limestone, we emphasize a good green background for carrying power.

Often it is difficult for an arranger to cut off the long stems of beautiful specimens, but don't be intimidated. Some blossoms must be placed at different heights in order to achieve the desired effect, so their stems must be sacrificed. Many altar guilds say to us that we can do that as our flowers do not go to the sick. It is true that our altar arrangements remain in place as long as the flowers are fresh so that they may be enjoyed by the thousands of visitors who tour or worship in Washington Cathedral. However, we do sometimes have a few leftover flowers which will not last through a second weekend. We have found that an ill staff member or a volunteer appreciates a few flowers tastefully arranged even more than a few loose flowers. We save plastic margarine bowls and used oasis for this purpose. This compact arrangement is much more suitable for a hospital room or bedside table than a few isolated long stems.

The following few remaining hints applicable to all types of flower arranging should be helpful:

1) Study the material to be used before beginning. With a design firmly in mind proceed with confidence! Changing one's mind causes overhandling and worries the flowers to death. Of course, some adjustment may be necessary when the arrangements are viewed in place, but the less the flowers are handled the longer they will last.

2) When using oasis the perforated side should be toward the front, following the manufacturer's code. Be sure to double check that no stems have been pushed all the way through the back of the oasis. If a stem has been placed incorrectly in the oasis, never use

the same hole to reposition it. An air pocket may remain to rob the flower of water.

3) For added interest and beauty use some of the flowers in profile as well as face on. Look for the natural curve of stems and incorporate them into your arrangement.

4) Unless planning mass color for a specific purpose, such as an "Easter sunrise," keep the arrangement loose and airy so that a "robin can fly through."

In some churches, because of the architecture and design of the sanctuary, all of the preceding premises may not be applicable—i.e. the cross may be very large and/or hanging on the wall, or it may rest on a raised footing or tabernacle; the altar may be free-standing with no retable; sometimes the retable may be small and/or laden with brass candlesticks or candelabra. The Eucharistic candles belong on the holy table for all services. In other instances the reredos is so elaborately carved or painted that confusion results with arrangements of any size.

Choose a quiet weekday and sit alone to study possibilities. Forget, momentarily, preconceived ideas and methods. True, the church has been given a pair of memorial vases, but their donor should not expect them to be used every Sunday anymore than the donor of a frontal for Advent expects it used for Pentecost. As one does not use the same container for the dining room table each night when the family gathers for dinner, so one should not be confined to the same containers at the holy table of the Lord.

Now study the area available for the beauty of nature. Could the reredos be framed? Could separate panels be underscored with a low retable arrangement? Is the only answer a pedestal or a pair of free-standing arrangements? Let your imagination and enthusiasm inspire you to create the loveliest arrangements for your God and your fellow worshippers—and have fun!

V

VASES and COMPOTES

Most churches have inherited a pair of Victorian narrow-necked vases whose small opening at the top have forced altar guilds to cope with an almost impossible task. The container's characteristic narrow neck confines the arranger primarily to an upward line, thus denying nature's balance between height and width. Skillfully executed, with the use of auxiliary mechanics, arrangements done in the traditional narrow-necked vase can be stunning. There are two techniques which we have found successful in overcoming the limitations of the flower arranger's nightmare.

MECHANICS 1

First a pinholder is dropped into the bottom of each vase. Next carve a soaked block of oasis to fit the narrow neck with several inches protruding above the lip of the vase. A bamboo garden stake is then pressed through the oasis into the pinholder below. For extra security a second small stake is inserted horizontally to support the width of the arrangement. The flowers then may be placed in the oasis. Great care should be taken to (a) prevent the oasis from crumbling by limiting the quantity of material and the number of thick stems. The oasis can support fewer stock and gladioli than carnations, sweetheart roses and Baker fern; (b) carefully place the flowers, as repeated changing of stems will destroy the oasis; (c) prevent overcrowding of the oasis by inserting only that length of stem necessary to support the material; (d) counterbalance the weight of the flowers in front by hanging strips of lead over the back lip of the vase.

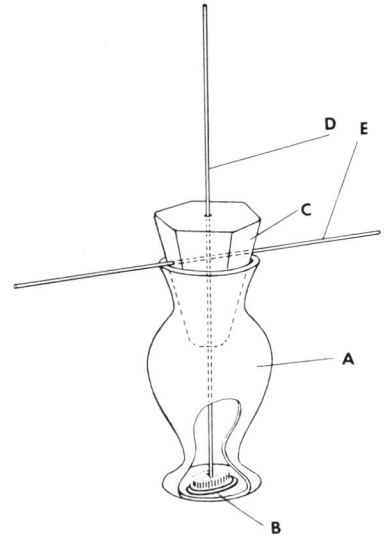

Mechanics 1 for a narrow necked vase (A) require a pinholder (B) dropped to the bottom, a carved piece of oasis (C) set into the neck, a vertical bamboo stake (D) thrust through the oasis into the pinholders and a horizontal stake (E) pushed through the oasis at the level of the lip of the vase.

MECHANICS 2 BEEHIVE

These mechanics, which we have dubbed the beehive, require a treated terra cotta or ceramic saucer, oasis, a wire hanging basket and adhesive floral tape. Used in varying dimensions the beehive is the basic mechanics for vases and pedestal arrangements of all sizes. For up to a twelve inch high, narrow-necked vase use an eight inch terra cotta saucer, such as one may purchase in any garden supply shop, painted on the outside with clear shellac or green paint, or sprayed thoroughly with a plastic sealer. A soaked block of oasis is placed in a standing position in the center of the saucer. The top third is carved off and sliced into four sections. Set these pieces around the original center block, and place an inverted wire hanging basket over them. The basket then is secured to the treated saucer with strips of adhesive floral tape. The beehive is ready to be set on top of the vase for arranging. As the front weight of the flowers increases, place counterbalancing weights in the back of the saucer for stability. Once the mechanics are constructed, and before the placement of any material, the arranger must remember to use flowers to form the outline against a dark background, or a heavy outline of greens against a light background, in order to make the arrangement stand out from its setting. At the cathedral we usually work against a limestone reredos, therefore use a heavy green outline. For a dark background proceed as with the greens, but use the flowers as the line material.

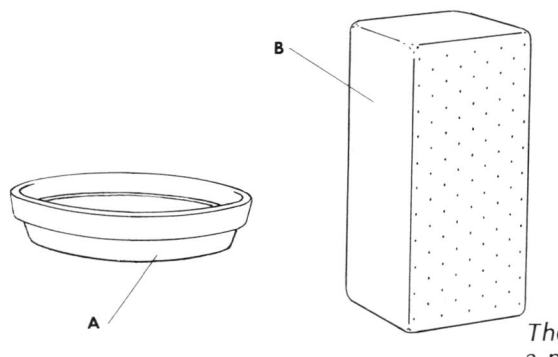

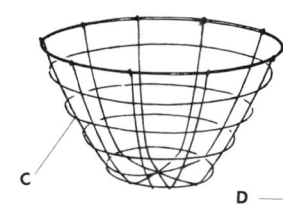

The requirements for Mechanics 2 for a narrow necked vase are an eight inch terra cotta saucer (A), a block of oasis (B), an eight inch wire hanging basket (C) and adhesive floral tape (D).

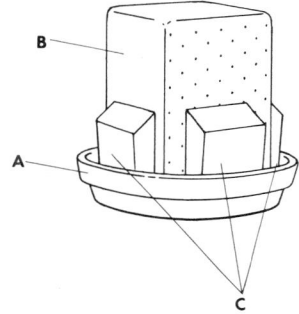

In the saucer (A) the block of oasis (B) is placed. When the top third of the oasis is carved off and sliced into quarters. Each fourth is placed around the block (C).

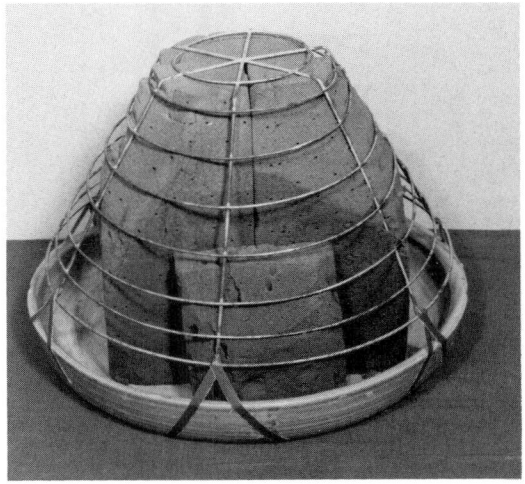

In using Mechanics 1 for a matched pair, one begins by choosing two similar stems of greens, as straight and as full as possible. Place each stem in the oasis directly in front of the upright bamboo stake. Fasten the stem to the stake with a small piece of twistem. For the horizontal line choose four stems as closely matching as possible. Insert these into the oasis at each horizontal stake and secure them. Fill in the areas between, keeping the greens toward the back of the oasis, and selecting the various lengths of green necessary to form an outline resembling a triangle whose sides bow inward. When treating vases this outline has a natural grace which the round ball, semicircle or the straight-sided triangle does not. The graceful bowed sides are aesthetically more pleasing to the eye and appropriate in flower arranging. When the background is completed the flower placement goes quickly.

Choose a matching pair of "spike-type" flowers, such as delphiniums, snapdragons or gladioli, and cut them slightly shorter than the greens. These should be inserted into the oasis at a slightly forward angle just in front of the vertical green of each vase. When viewed from the congregation this angle positioning will give depth to the arrangement, and make the stalks look straight instead of appearing flat, or as if they might fall backwards. Then, as with the greens, choose four matching flowers for the horizontal outline. The remaining spikes are then selected, cut, and placed alternately in each vase, creating mirror images of each other.

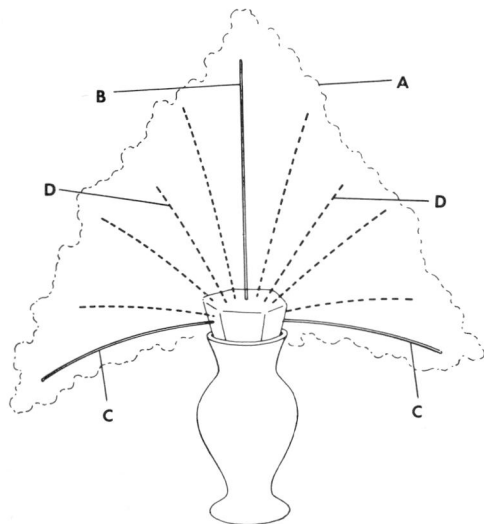

With the green background in place (A), the flower placement begins with the vertical spike line (B), then the addition of the pair of horizontals (C) and finally the spikes between (D).

While stunning arrangements can be executed with spike flowers alone, one can create equally effective arrangements using what we call "round-type" flowers. These flowers are those whose blossom, or mass of blossoms, grows at the end of a stem, such as chrysanthemums, tulips, Queen Anne's lace and roses. The individual nature of the round-type flowers allows the arranger the freedom to place each blossom in one of many attitudes, from full-face to profile, in order to exploit the beauty of each specimen.

A beautiful arrangement of round-type flowers is graceful and satisfying. When spikes and rounds are mixed, however, the result is a stunning arrangement which has all the vitality of spikes and the softness of rounds. Once the background of greens is completed one begins, as for a spike arrangement, by placing the three initial spikes in the oasis to form the boundary of the triangle. These strong lines give a feeling of dynamic boldness and vitality to which one adds the soft, graceful curves of the rounds. The large round blossoms are used to establish the focal point. They are placed in the lower center of the triangle at varying depths to create dimension. Care is taken to ensure that the bottom line is staggered, and that the stems of all of the focal blossoms emanate from the central root ball. The remaining smaller blossoms and buds are used to fill in the rest of the triangle.

The method just described is the basic procedure for the arranging of all vases. When more flowers are available, particularly those which have thicker stems, Mechanics 1 is no longer feasible, as the oasis will crumble. In this case we use the beehive described in Mechanics 2. When this technique is utilized the side bamboo stakes are eliminated since the stems of the lower greens and flowers are supported by the wire basket rims. One may decide to retain the upright bamboo if the greens are not straight, or the stems are too weak to be self-supporting. Having determined the necessary mechanics for the materials to be used, the arranging proceeds as before. The value of the beehive to the arranger cannot be stressed enough because it relieves any fear of crumbling and allows for a greater variety of design. Whether using the traditional triangle, or creating other designs such as the crescent, or Hogarth curve, the arranger can depend upon the security of the beehive.

The mechanics described in Mechanics 1 and 2 have released the arranger from the confines of the narrow-necked Victorian vase. More recent designs of altar vases, however, feature a flared mouth which facilitates arranging. Even though these wider mouths do help somewhat in simplifying arranging, we have found that the use of Mechanics 1 is simpler, safer, and more effective.

Akin to the more modern wide-mouthed vase is the footed compote. A pair of compotes gives the same type of arrangement feeling as a pair of vases, but has the characteristics of being wider, and having a lower focal point. This is important because the width allows the arranger to use more flowers, and achieve a looser, larger and less stylized arrangement. The lower focal point permits more latitude for height without exceeding the measurement of the cross arm of the cross.

Mechanics for compotes resemble the technique of Mechanics 1 for vases. A pinholder is secured to the bottom of a clean, dry compote. A block of oasis is forced onto the stocking-covered pinholder. The height of the oasis varies according to the length of the material to be arranged, and the depth of the container. In all cases the oasis should be several inches above the lip of the compote to permit a graceful downward line when the stems are inserted from the bottom and sides or at various slight angles off the horizontal. As in the technique for Mechanics 1, the vertical and horizontal bamboo stakes are now added, unless the materials to be used are sturdy enough to stand alone. The placing of the materials then follows the same basic steps as those used when arranging in vases.

The execution of bouquets in compotes and wide-mouthed and narrow-necked vases, whose confining shapes heretofore have limited and often frustrated the arranger, takes on new and exciting dimensions with the aid of supplementary mechanics. These two simple techniques release the arranger from the fetters of these containers and allow unlimited freedom of creativity to devise beautiful and gratifying arrangements for both the arranger and the worshipper.

VI

BOXES

In Washington Cathedral we use boxes as altar flower containers more often than vases and compotes combined. Not only do boxes have the advantage of giving the arranger more latitude for display and expression, but they also lend themselves to sturdier mechanics. The marvellously simple shape makes them invaluable because with these containers it is possible to construct arrangements for placement in pairs in any position from the outside corners of the retable to the sides of the cross. Boxes also may be used singly to adorn the cross, pulpit, font and almost any appropriate area in the church. The choice of placement determines the design, and each design creates a different feeling. For instance, in the spring when showery branches of golden forsythia and banks of sunny daffodils grow in profusion, an arranger may decide to use them on Sunday in boxes on the outside corners of the retable with the long curved branches of forsythia growing out of the massed focal point of daffodils partially to frame the reredos and give the feeling of spring and new life. The following Sunday a more traditional triangular shape placed equidistant between the cross and candles, using the less flamboyant branches of forsythia interspersed with the daffodils gives an appreciation of each blossom and a feeling of order and tranquility.

Arranging flowers in a pair of handsome, well-polished brass or silver boxes is a luxury few churches can afford. A number of inexpensive alternatives make fine containers. Brass-wash planter boxes in varying lengths are available in some gardening centers. A local sheet metal shop can fabricate a pair of boxes which can be painted to blend into the retable or reredos. Even aluminum bread pans or small plastic flower boxes make excellent substitutes. Regardless of the fabric of the boxes, they are a welcome addition to the container collection.

The mechanics for boxes vary slightly according to the size chosen. A brass-wash planter box usually measures three-and-one-half inches wide. This simplifies the basic mechanics because this width is the same as that of a block of oasis. Since the sides of the oasis are firmly supported against the sides of the box, only the ends need securing. In twelve to fourteen inch long boxes center a soaked block of oasis, perforations toward the front, and place a No. 9 oval pinholder at a 45° angle in the front corner of each end of the box. Grasp the pair of pinholders in one of the boxes and rotate them simultaneously inward until the front end of each pinholder is wedged into the corners of the box, and the other ends are firmly implanted into the block of oasis. After repeating the wedging process for the other box they are ready for arranging.

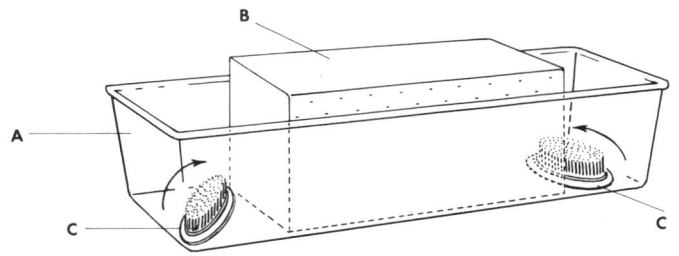

A planter box 14" x 3½" x 3½" (A) uses one block of oasis (B) and a pair of #9 pinholders (C). The pinholders are placed at a 45° angle into the front corners of the box, then rotated inward to wedge the oasis securely in place.

If the boxes are wider than three-and-one-half inches, and/or longer than fourteen inches, a different method is necessary. In this case the No. 9 pinholders, covered with pieces of nylon stocking, are secured to the ends of each box with floral clay. Impale the soaked oasis, with its side firmly against the back of the box, on the pinholders. For longer boxes a supplementary portion of a block of oasis is necessary, and the addition of a third pinholder at the bottom of the joint gives more stability. The box never should be completely filled with oasis since overloading hinders watering. Sometimes arrangers desire the extra security of narrow strips of adhesive floral tape to hold the oasis in place. NEVER fasten these to the outside of silver or brass containers as they mar the finish. Some planter boxes have liners to which tape can be secured. Tape can be fastened to the inside of any box if one has not allowed the oasis to dampen it. When the ends of the tape are reinforced with a cross piece of tape they will remain in position.

Before contructing additional mechanics the arranger must pause to decide where the pair of boxes will be placed because where the arrangements are situated determines the general design. When the boxes are placed equidistant between the cross and candlesticks they are treated as triangles, or open fans, with the height in the center of each. They also may be open crescents with the low point at or near the center and sides curving upward. However, if they are close to the cross, or at the outside corners of the retable, the pair of boxes will be arranged as right-angled triangles either facing or opposing each other.

Further mechanics security for a box (A) with oasis (B) impaled on a pinholder (C) may be achieved by a strip of adhesive floral tape (D) twisted (E) to adhere to the inside of the box. This is reinforced by a cross piece of the tape (F).

For a box 18" long (A) two #9 pinholders (B) are secured by floral clay (C) at each end of the box and a third secured pinholder at the spot where one full block of oasis (D) and a portion of a second (E) converge. The oasis (D & E) blocks are then impaled onto the pinholders.

33

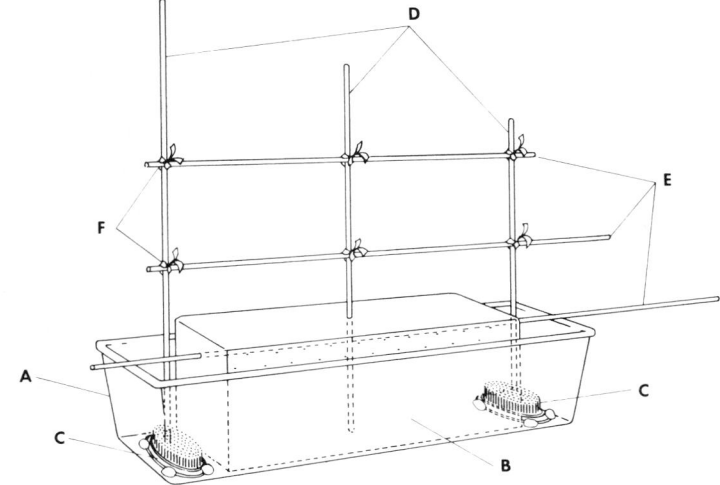

Supplementary mechanics for a box 14" long (A) involves placing the block of oasis (B), on a pair of #9 pinholders secured by floral clay, then fastening the three vertical bamboo stakes (D) into the pinholders and oasis and finally adding the three horizontal supports (E). The lowers of these is thrust through the oasis at the box rim level and the top two are secured to the verticals with twistem (F).

The supplementary support for the triangle and fan design resembles that used for vases or compotes. Cut a green bamboo stake slightly lower than the cross arm measurement to establish the vertical line in the center of the oasis. Thrust the second bamboo stake horizontally through the oasis at the box rim level to support the outside dimensions.

The right-angled designs, often used for festival arrangements or for heavy-stemmed material, may require a bamboo framework for additional security. Place a bamboo stake, which has been cut slightly lower than the cross arm measurement, vertically into the corner pinholder. Place a second stake, which is somewhat shorter, into the center back of the oasis, and secure a still shorter third stake into the opposite pinholder. Three horizontal stakes are then placed. The first is thrust through the oasis at the box rim level. The other two are secured by twistem at successive levels across the three vertical stakes. Materials can be firmly held in place by attaching them to this framework with twistem. Armed with good mechanics, heavy-stemmed greens and flowers can be arranged in the sacristy and moved to the altar without fear of the oasis breaking apart or the whole arrangement toppling over.

Alternatives to oasis mechanics are those which utilize pinholders and chicken wire. They may be used when arranging both flowers and greens, but we always use them when arranging foliage only. (Refer to Chapter VIII for the steps of these alternative mechanics.)

Just as the support mechanics for the pair of center triangular designs is contructed in a manner similar to those in vases and compotes, so the placement of materials follows a like process. Choose the vertical and outside greens and fill in the triangle. Then add the flowers in the same order. The finished pair, while similar to vases or compotes, has a longer and lower horizontal line. For a slightly more modern version of this triangle, consider the position of the rootball a few inches off center toward the outside end of each box. A pair of asymetrical triangles is *dramatic* when arranged solely with spikes thrust at quite dynamic angles.

When the boxes are to be placed close to the cross a right-angled triangle is most effective. In this design the rootball is located in the corner of each box next to the base of the cross. Begin by selecting two pieces of green as straight and dense as possible. Put them into the inside pinholders and attach them with twistem to the bamboo uprights. Next, the pair of outside greens is chosen and inserted into the oasis for the horizontal line. The outline of the triangle then is solidly filled in toward the back of the oasis. Anchor stems to the framework as necessary. For placement of flowers, select two spike blossoms which resemble each other as nearly as possible in size, straightness of stem, and density. Clip the stems to identical lengths, shorter than the greens, and place one in each pinholder on the inside end of the boxes. Secure these to the bamboo if needed. Select a second pair for the outside dimension. With each succeeding pair keep in mind that the blossoms must be mirror images of each other and inserted at a slightly forward angle. It is essential to place all stems so that they appear to emanate from the rootball to ensure a correct spike line.

Sometimes the round material, such as carnations, chrysanthemums, tulips or daisies, is kept low and close to the inside corners of the boxes to form a focal point at the base of the cross. A different, freer feeling is achieved when these flowers are interspersed among the spikes. When the arrangements are put in place, close to each side of the cross, we occasionally add a few pieces of greens in the back corners of the boxes to extend behind the cross. This has the effect of linking the pair into a single arrangement and making the cross stand out in greater prominence.

If the same pair is switched, and each box placed at the outside corners of the retable, the design effect is completely different. Instead of leaving the vertical lines straight, the arranger should add a few greens to give a more graceful curved line. In this position a pleasing variation results when the hypotenuse is bowed slightly inward.

35

The flower arranging course offered at Washington Cathedral during Lent devotes more than half of the workshop sessions to the use of boxes. This prepares the apprentice members of our altar guild to handle flower arranging in this most commonly used container on a weekly basis as well as for major festivals. (See Chapters X, XI and XII.)

Boxes are used in many ways to create unusual and interesting designs. If your flower committee has no boxes, we urge you to purchase a pair of bread pans and experiment on your own with this versatile container. You will be amazed to find that you have added a new horizon in altar arranging for your church.

VII

PEDESTALS

Pedestal arrangements are very effective whether created singly or in pairs. Their versatility of placement, choice of materials and designs makes them both exciting and challenging for the arranger. Since they can be so dramatic, free-standing arrangements rarely fail to elicit admiration.

Pedestals produce striking results in many locations including those by a fixed or free-standing altar, inside the altar rail, flanking the rood screen, near the pulpit or lectern, against a pillar, at the entrance of a chapel or near the font. An examination of your church will probably reveal a number of other locations where a pedestal arrangement would be equally spectacular. In choosing such locations keep firmly in mind the ritual of your church, the movements of the clergy and choir and the sight lines of the congregation and participants. The flowers must never impede any of these.

Selection of a base is the first consideration. Here the choice is almost limitless. The size of the base is governed by its location. A massive stand is unsuitable near a delicately wrought lectern just as a dainty, short pedestal is lost when placed next to a towering pulpit.

Obtaining a pedestal need not be a difficult or expensive task. For a large stand visit a local wrecking company or junk yard to find a front porch pillar or a stairway balustrade. These may be painted to blend into the background, or antiqued to give the appearance of marble or wrought iron. At a brick yard you can purchase a twenty-three inch high square terra cotta chimney flue and paint it to resemble stone. For a more delicate shaft, use a wooden or wrought iron plant stand. Some specialty lumberyards carry milled pieces of wood which, when screwed together, become uprights for bookshelves. Several of these put together to the desired height with a sturdy footing and platform top attached make a fine pedestal which unscrews for easy storage. An old forgotten candlestick which may be tucked up in the attic of a parishioner will take on a new role when brought into the church and slightly modified.

We were given a pair of antique pewter candlesticks, thirty-eight inches high, for use as flower pedestals. To adapt these the following steps were taken:

1. The pointed prong, meant to support the candle, was cut off one inch above its base.
2. An eight-inch-diameter disc of one-inch thick plywood was fashioned, and a hole equal in diameter to the prong stub was drilled through the center.
3. Fitting the disc onto the prong, it becomes the platform for the beehive mechanics.

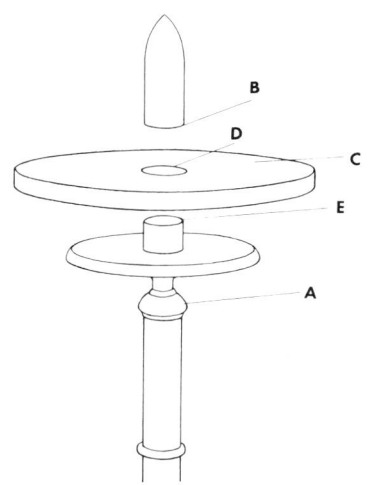

To adapt our 38" high candlesticks (A) for pedestals, we cut off the prongs meant to support the candles (B). An eight inch disc of 1" plywood (C) was made with a 1¼" hole in the center (D) to fit over the cut off prong (E).

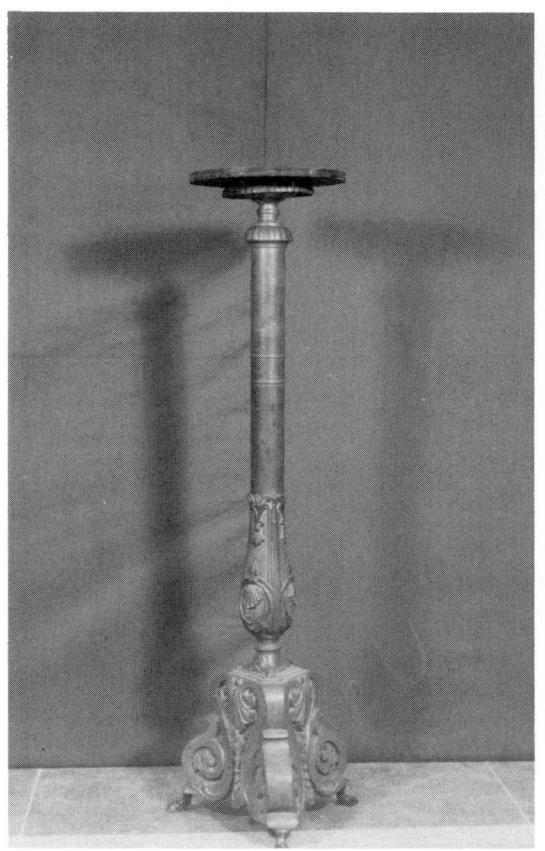

Some years later, after seeing how the pewter candlesticks were adapted to serve as a pedestal for a free-standing arrangement, an admirer of the cathedral sent a pair of forty-five inch high wrought iron candlesticks to the altar guild. Nothing was done to the candlesticks themselves. We had sheet metal pans, similar to ring molds, made to fit down over the candle socket and rest on the drip rim (bobeche). After filling the pans with oasis we arrange flowers into a wreath which surrounds the lighted candle. A beautiful unit in itself, it is particularly effective during a service when the candle is lighted. For this reason we use them primarily for special occasions.

For a festival when baptisms are not scheduled, and the priest or minister

approves, the font becomes a pedestal for a striking arrangement. Do not use the basin as the container. Line it with plastic for protection and construct proper mechanics in a separate container which can be put into the font.

Having chosen the site and the properly scaled stand for that area, the next step is to prepare the mechanics. For an arrangement such as our pewter candlesticks hold we use glazed ceramic saucers. A terra cotta plant saucer may be substituted, but it must be treated on the outside so that moisture cannot penetrate to loosen the adhesive tape. Three new blocks of soaked standard oasis are placed vertically on the saucer. Never layer oasis as the block on top will not absorb enough water from the under block to keep the

40

stems wet. We then carve several used pieces for fill around the vertical three so that the fourteen inch inverted wire hanging basket is entirely packed with oasis and will not shift. The basket then is taped securely to the saucer. We take great care to keep the outside of the saucer dry so the tape will stick. In the interest of economy, the adhesive tape strips may be split lengthwise.

These same mechanics would be used for any size base, the variables being only the diameter of the saucers and wire baskets (eight to sixteen inches), and the amount of oasis needed to fill them. We have found aluminum and plastic dishpans practical for deep pedestal bases such as the font. However, if the oasis is not high enough to extend sufficiently above the rim, the bottom of the pan is lined with pieces of brick to elevate the oasis blocks. The wire basket then is secured to the sides. If greens or flowers are too short, or a higher top line is desired, two additional bits of mechanics can be employed.

To the top of the completed beehive add a cemetery urn which has legs of bamboo stakes firmly taped to it. The stakes are thrust into the oasis, and the urn taped to the top of the wire basket. For an exceptionally top-heavy addition it would be advisable to line the saucer with stocking-covered pinholders before beginning the beehive. The bamboo legs of the cemetery urn can be pushed through the oasis into the pinholders for greater stability. If only several stems need lengthening prepare a few florist water picks or test tubes by taping them to bamboo stakes. These will be ready to fill and insert into your arrangement.

The pedestal is placed in the desired location and the beehive set upon it. If there is the least doubt as to stability of the beehive on the pedestal, tape the saucer to the pedestal platform. The beehive must be firmly anchored to prevent a catastrophe such as we had when the sleeve of a surplice brushed the flowers and brought the arrangement tumbling down in the middle of a service.

Before beginning the actual arrangement spread a dust sheet, newspapers or plastic around the pedestal to prevent staining the floor or carpet. With the mechanics prepared and the pedestal properly placed the arranging begins. This will be a three-quarter arrangement since it is viewed from three sides only, the back being against a surface, such as the lectern. The fourth side of the arrangement will have greens covering the mechanics, but no flowers. Arranging will proceed in much the same order as preparing an altar triangle, but usually on a much larger scale. The top piece of green is placed well back in the beehive and not in the center top. Otherwise the profile line will be spoiled. Next, the outside line pieces are chosen and inserted, bracing them against the wire basket. These pieces should be selected carefully to afford a most graceful downward flowing line. Complete the background green line, remembering to keep it slightly concave so that the finished arrangement will not have a "ball" effect. The spike material is now placed inside the green background. Be sure to keep in mind the location of the rootball. It is often tempting to add a downward line stem at such an angle that its source would be the top of the beehive. If snapdragons are being used, remember that by the following day the tips are likely to have turned upward. This characteristic can make the snapdragon appear cheerful and uplifting, however, they may appear to be in conflict with a design which stresses the straight line. Once the spike outline is complete, begin placing the round type flowers. If the stems of materials such as carnations or majestic daisies appear flimsy, they should be wired before adding them. Finish the arrangement by hiding the mechanics, basket and saucer with bits of green. This should be done carefully as pedestals are viewed close at hand as well as from the distance.

In the English tradition, a single pedestal arrangement is ideal when using materials from the garden and roadside since gathering enough material to arrange a matched pair is next to impossible.

In executing a matched pair, the arrangers first decide the line and dimensions. If stems are cut and placed in pairs the work is simplified. Although they never will be perfect images of each, they will give the illusion of matching when the line and placement of color is as similar in each pair as is possible. The arrangers must constantly step back and view the pair while in the process of arranging.

Slightly more difficult to execute is a pedestal arrangement which is meant to be viewed from all sides, such as one located close to a free-standing altar in the midst of the congregation. The two most vital differences to remember in working are: (1) The rootball is located in the bottom center of the beehive, and (2) the arranging should be carried on evenly on all sides. This second point presents no problem if the work is done by layers in a circular manner. For the top spike try a single full snapdragon, or clump three gladioli to face around. Depending on the size of the arrangement, pick out three to five stems of similar weight in blossom. Cut all these stems the same length but shorter than the top flowers. Insert these stems around as the first layer from the top, being sure to avoid placing them in a straight ring. Then select the next grouping, cut the stems, and place them in the second layer level. Continue these steps until the final lower line is finished. Before beginning it is advisable to count out the number of stems and determine the number of pieces available per layer. Always leave a few stems in reserve for filling unintentional holes after the layers have been placed. Exercise careful selection of color and size of flowers for an all around pedestal arrangement as there can be no heavy green background to back up the flowers. In this case, the flowers stand on their own with the greens used only for mechanics and stem cover.

When the pedestal is completed and the debris cleaned up, one more vital step remains. All arrangements should be given a final topping up with water, this is essential for arrangements made with beehive mechanics. The beehive always is watered from the top by dribbling a trickle slowly over the entire surface. This is necessary as oasis does not have enough osmosis to draw up water from the submerged bottom to the top of the block. The saucers are shallow, and hold little water. If the oasis sheds the water too quickly for total saturation, use a baster to remove the water from the saucer and trickle more clean water over the top. In extremely dry weather we have experimented by covering the oasis with florist foil or sphagnum moss, but we have found the results not much better than careful and thorough daily watering.

Since many arrangers never have created a pedestal design, an easy way to gain confidence is to start with a three-quarter basic triangle arrangement consisting of material of a single color. This needs no extra mechanics added to the beehive. Perhaps the most dramatic for a first venture is a combination of red gladioli and red carnations. After you feel comfortable with the size and mechanics, move on to a design of different colored flowers like yellow gladioli with bronze and yellow Red Rover chrysanthemums. Then try a Hogarth curve instead of the basic triangle. Soon you will find yourself thinking of all sorts of effects which you can achieve when using many kinds of materials in combination in varying designs. You will look forward to the next time it is your turn to create a pedestal arrangement for your church.

VIII

FOLIAGE

Anyone visiting Washington Cathedral during the four weeks of Advent or in the months of July and August will find arrangements on the majority of the altars created with foliage. Except for an occasional memorial, funeral or summer wedding when flowers are used, the weekly altar arrangements consist of a variety of greens.

An arrangement of foliage can be as beautiful and impressive as one done with flowers. The key is in the contrast of form, color and texture provided in the selection and combination of materials. With an appreciation of foliage, and a recognition of the unique character of leaves, arranging takes on a new dimension. Fresh, crisp plant material of contrasting textures, and subtle colorations provides unlimited possibilities for imaginative and distinctive designs. In addition, many garden plants, berries and seed heads help give variety and interest to an all green arrangement. Houseplants can be a splendid source of greens as is material gleaned from the wayside and stream banks. Grasses, including grains, reeds and sedges gathered before they reach maturity will retain their lovely coloring. Evergreens are valuable because they can be used throughout the year. In the summer months they can be combined with deciduous material. Nature's talent for exquisite leaf design, its shape, veining and texture, gives us another dimension for contrast in an arrangement and should be accented. When individual leaves or clusters of leaves are chosen they almost always comprise the focal point of the arrangement. If a branch is selected for its line and leaf design, judicious pruning may be necessary to release selected leaves from the mass.

Color is an equally important element in the use of foliage. The success of the greens arrangement, where two or more materials are used, depends upon the selection of contrasting hues. Although most persons consider the category of greens to be boughs and stems of green leaves, this term embraces a wide spectrum of shades, hues and colors. Within the category of "green leaves", vegetation ranges from yellow-green to blue-green. Other leaves have variegated characteristics. Some plant leaves change from green to a variety of different colors through the seasons, and a few, such as Dusty Miller, are not green at all. A partial list of foliage by color for our climate, Zone VII, is included in Appendix 2.

The summer material is cut several days in advance of arranging. Older branches are selected as new growth usually will not survive conditioning. To help condition the leaves, as well as remove dirt and dust, a good idea is to submerge the branches in the bathtub overnight. The husband of one of our arrangers complains that before his wife's weekend on duty he must take a shower because the master bathtub always is filled with magnolia from her "cathedral cutting tree."

After soaking overnight the stems of branches are scraped of bark, split, and left to condition in deep water. Certain greens require special conditioning. Recommendations for the conditioning of these are described in Appendix 1.

Summer greens offer a wide variety of materials. A pedestal might be designed with long and graceful branches of mock orange, combined with golden flecked aucuba and accented with the deep gold of yarrow. We do occasionally combine dried materials with fresh foliage. A box arrangement could contain a dark green outline of euonymous with light leafy flowerets of laurel as accent. Our Children's Chapel altar might be decorated with a variety of dainty, sweet smelling herbs. The prolific ivy of our area often is added to designs for graceful trailing lines. Variegated materials, such as hosta and liriope are prized for accent.

Advent greens are limited to those species not affected by frost. We can count on conifers of various types, ligustrum, magnolia, cherry laurel, ilex, aucuba and other hardy materials. We try to include some of the fragrant evergreens which herald the Christmas season. The Advent wreaths are fashioned from arbor-vitae which will hold through the four Sundays. This evergreen usually dries but never sheds. One faithful altar guild instructor waits to prune her shrubs until late November so that we may have the arbor-vitae for the wreaths.

When Christmas falls on a Monday or Tuesday, the greens for the fourth Sunday in Advent are designed and arranged so that they serve as the background for the festive Christmas decor. Some of our most successful stand-bys are noble fir, blue spruce, green and variegated holly and magnolia. Having the mechanics constructed and the background in place, the guild members may return on Christmas Eve only to add flowers and finish the arrangements, thus giving them more time for personal Christmas preparations.

The same principles and elements of design are used in the arranging of foliage as in floral arrangements. Since at the cathedral, they are meant to last for several weeks, we employ alternative mechanics to ensure greater water consumption. To set up boxes for greens we line the bottoms of the pair with pinholders. A length of one-inch chicken wire three times the width of the box is cut from the roll with wire cutters. The chicken wire is then folded into thirds which will give triple support for the stems. The ends of the wire are crumpled under to fit into the ends of the boxes, taking great care that the sharp cut ends do not scratch the containers. The arranger may want to wear an old pair of gloves to protect the hands.

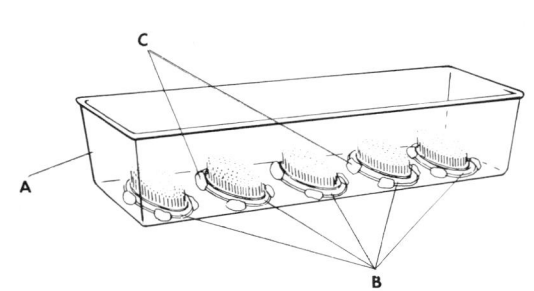

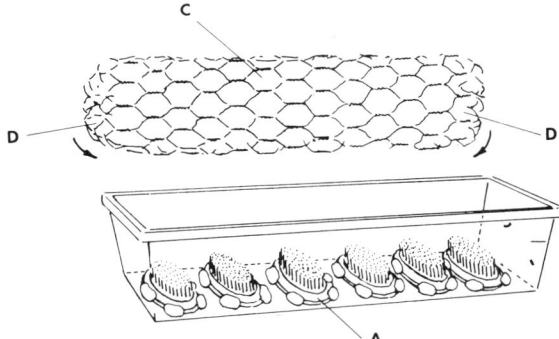

For arranging a 14" box (A) without oasis #9 pinholders (B) are secured to the bottom of the box with dabs of floral clay (C).

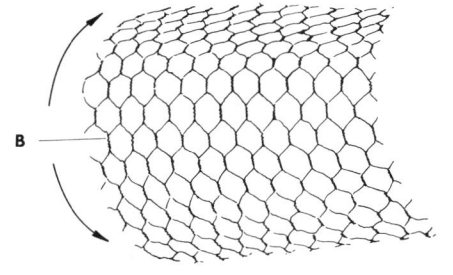

Complete the mechanics for the 14" box filled with pinholders (A) by cutting one inch chicken wire (B) into a piece approximately 12" x 16" and fold into thirds. Take this roll of wire (C) and fold in the ends (D) to fit the box.

46

Arranging may begin by inserting the upright green through the chicken wire into the pinholders. The horizontal or bosomy foliage should be threaded through the layers of wires. Because some of these horizontal stems may be just below the rim of the box always keep the water level up to the brim. These same steps can be applied to vases and compotes. For pedestals and standards, however, oasis still is used in the beehives.

Greens arranged with these mechanics can last for three or four weeks with only minor replacements if a few precautions are observed:

(1) Use only crisp, fresh foliage which has been properly conditioned.

(2) Use only pinholders in a good state and coated chicken wire. Since rusty water can be as destructive to plant material as slime, purchase green painted chicken wire from a florist supply house. There is a superior plastic coated wire, but it is hard to find.

(3) The water level is kept topped up. Use one tablespoon of bleach to a gallon of water to retard decay.

(4) Once a week syphon all water from the container with a baster, and add new bleach water.

Foliage arrangements not only enhance the place of worship and give a fresh lift to the spirit of the worshippers, but also present an on-going challenge to the arranger to turn the everyday materials of gardens, hedges and byways into an acceptable offering to God.

IX

SPECIAL SERVICES

Duties of the altar guild include not only arranging flowers for regularly prescribed weekly services but also occasional supplementary services scheduled throughout the year. These special services include the sacraments of Holy Matrimony, Holy Baptism, Confirmation and Ordination, as well as funerals, dedications, installation of clergy, vestry or elders, Rogation Day blessing of the fields, Christmas pageants and concerts.

WEDDINGS

One of our happiest duties is arranging the flowers for a wedding. It always is a pleasure to interview each bridal couple or bride and her parents. The infectious joy and excitement in the preparation for this all-important ceremony in a young couple's life invades the altar guild office.

Some brides arrive with definite ideas of flowers and the colors they prefer, while others come looking for suggestions they can carry to their personal florist for wedding party bouquets and reception arrangements.

Most brides prefer altar arrangements to the second option of pedestals at the altar rail. These are the only types of wedding church flowers permitted at the Washington Cathedral. We feel the Gothic beauty needs no other adornment. The couple will come to unite in the sacrament of Holy Matrimony; therefore, as for other services, the cross must be the focal point. This ruling was made because on one occasion the bride ordered the sanctuary banked in baskets of flowers so that the altar and cross were scarcely visible. It became a production rather than a religious service. This type of display should be saved for the reception.

The bride is given her choice of altar containers. She may select vases, compotes or boxes. Then she chooses the flowers and greens from a list of materials available on the date of her wedding. The most popular in white are snapdragons or gladioli for the spike materials, and carnations or chrysanthemums for the round type.

The addition of some color or use of mixed color bouquet has become increasingly popular. The bride may want to accent the color of her attendants' gowns by adding Sonia roses, yellow tulips or pink carnations to a white arrangement of snapdragons and starburst chrysanthemums.

A mixed spring wedding arrangement might consist of yellow and white snapdragons, pink peonies, yellow and white Marguerite daisies and a few red carnations to give the final sparkling touch.

In the hot summer months some brides prefer the coolness of an all-white arrangement. Others select the vibrant summer colors of zinnias, celosia and marigolds.

For fall weddings the golds and bronzes of chrysanthemums are favorites.

Sometimes we are asked to add a sentimental touch such as pyracantha from the side yard of the family home, ivy which was rooted from the bride's mother's wedding bouquet, or a special flower which the bridegroom often gave to the bride during courtship. For one Hawaiian wedding the bride had leis flown in to use instead of bouquets. She had a few birds of paradise sent as well. These were added as an accent to a white arrangement.

If the wedding takes place following a major festival such as Thanksgiving, Christmas or Easter when the festival arrangements are still in place, these flowers must be used as the altar decorations for the wedding. Since she is required to use these flowers, they become our gift to the bride. All other wedding flowers are left upon the altar as the bride's gift for the Sunday service.

BAPTISMS

Another of our duties in the altar guild is arranging flowers for the service of Holy Baptism. This service may be a private ceremony or incorporated into the regular Sunday service. The type of service chosen determines the location and treatment of the flowers. For some families, the baptism of the child is a private affair. Therefore they wish only the family members, Godparents and a few very close friends to witness the baby's entry into the Christian community. Since this service would involve only the baptistry or font area, the altar guild often arranges special flowers for that location. For the christening of a child a pedestal arrangement of delicate flowers is particularly charming. These might include snapdragons, Marguerite daisies, miniature carnations and baby's breath with Baker fern and tendrils of dainty ivy. A box set at the base of the font is most effective when arranged with garden flowers or weeds and wildfowers such as a child might pick and bring home. The flower committee might consider arranging a partial wreath of dried flowers to be placed on the rim of the font. This has the advantage of being prepared at one's leisure and ready for repeated use. Children's Chapel in Washington Cathedral is most popular for private baptisms. Since they often are scheduled when the weekly flowers have faded, or the altar contains only foliage, our dried wreath provides instant flowers at a moment's notice.

A fourteen inch styrofoam wreath form is used. One quarter of it is carved away leaving plenty of room for the arm of the clergyman performing the baptism. The top, sides, and cut ends of the wreath are impaled with tiny dried materials such as miniature pink rose buds, light blue, yellow and white statice, bits of yellow goldenrod, short clipped stems of pink larkspur, white German statice and baby's breath. The effect is airy and childlike. The wreath is stored in a plastic trash bag with a bit of silica gel to retain its freshness and keep it dust free. To secure the wreath firmly to the rim of the font three or four dabs of floral clay are used on the bottom of the form.

Although private baptisms are popular, most churches incorporate them into the weekly service so that the whole congregation may welcome the new member or members. If the altar flowers have not already been provided by someone else as a memorial, the parents or sponsors may wish to give them as a gift of thanksgiving. When altar flowers are scheduled, however, and some additional floral display is desired at the font, the flowers in the font arrangement should co-ordinate with those on the altar. If the candidates for baptism are adults stronger colors can be used.

As in the ancient tradition, many churches hold group baptisms on Holy Saturday. Additional information on the decorating of the baptistry or font area can be found in Chapter XI, Easter.

FUNERALS AND MEMORIALS

Knowing the comfort that flowers provide for bereaved families, we in the altar guild find great satisfaction in preparing arrangements for funerals. If, before death, the deceased had specified the altar flowers desired at his funeral, the altar guild respects these wishes. On the other hand, if no pre-arrangement was made, we consult with the family regarding the appropriate flowers.

High Altar summer greens arrangements in cement bird baths: magnolia, hemlock and variegated hosta

summer greens box arrangements for Holy Spirit Chapel: green ti leaves, pink and green variegated ti and hosta

vesica frame Christmas arrangement in St. Mary's Chapel: greens, magnolia: flowers, bagged white poinsettia plants
photo: Barrett

High Altar at Christmas: frames and boxes: greens, Noble fir on cross frame, magnolia on side frames: flowers, bagged red poinsettia plants

Christmas pedestal arrangement for the High Altar sanctuary: greens, blue spruce: flowers, red gladioli, Bells of Ireland, bagged red poinsettia plants

Easter sunrise box arrangement for Resurrection Chapel: greens, ti leaves: flowers, yellow snap-dragons and Dutch iris, orange Mid-Century lilies
photo: Barrett

Easter box arrangements for Bethlehem Chapel: greens, aspidistra leaves: flowers, white snap-dragons and lilies

Easter pillar garlands in Bethlehem Chapel: greens, Baker fern: flowers, white statice, Fuji pom-pom chrysanthemums and gypsophilia

Thanksgiving box arrangements for War Memorial Chapel: greens, magnolia: dried material,
wheat, rolls and loaves of bread: treated materials, lemons and grapes

one of a pair of Thanksgiving arrangements for Bethlehem Chapel: styrofoam cone in compote:
greens, magnolia and arbor-vitae: dried materials, wheat and yarrow, treated material, gourds,
lemons, limes, kumquats and grapes
photo: Barrett

wrought iron pedestal/wicker cornucopia: greens, arbor-vitae and magnolia: treated materials, red oak leaves, apples, pineapples, artichokes, grapefruit, limes, lemons, oranges, strung cranberries, bananas, persimmons and grapes

Generally, if the deceased was quite old, the choice of flowers is all white. More and more, however, we are hearing "make it colorful," or "he loved yellow," or "she loved bright colors." Although white is the traditional color of the Resurrection, many feel bright colors also express the joy of our belief in life everlasting.

On the day of the funeral the altar guild member on duty places the altar arrangements. She calls the funeral director to inquire whether any floral tributes will be brought to the church. In Washington Cathedral we specify that only a few displays of fresh quality may be brought into the church. These are arranged around the sides and back of the chapel so that the cross with its altar flower arrangement remains the focal point. If sprays or baskets are sent directly to the cathedral the member on duty removes the cards and writes on the back a description of the arrangement such as "a fireside basket of pink and white gladioli, lavender chrysanthemums and white majestic daisies," or a "spray of red roses." This permits the family to thank the donors for specific flowers. We do not write on the card envelopes as they can become mixed or separated from the cards. The funeral director generally removes these flowers, although sometimes they are left for the altar guild's re-use.

DEDICATIONS

Since life does not end with death and the funeral, families and friends often give additions or renovations to the church in memory and thanksgiving for the life of loved ones. These gifts are dedicated in a separate service, or incorporated into a regularly scheduled service. Such gifts merit special recognition, and for these the altar guild often is requested to arrange flowers in addition to those on the altar. If the memorial is a movable one, such as a Bible, chalice or cross, it can be displayed with a crescent of flowers in front, or a frame of flowers behind. For a stationary gift, such as a stained glass window, or a new organ, a pedestal of flowers under the window or close to the console is appropriate. Regardless of the nature of the gift, the donor always appreciates being consulted on the choice of the flowers and their color.

Often dedications are planned to coincide with special services over which the bishop and other church dignitaries preside. These services include confirmation, ordination and the installation of a clergyman. Such festive occasions create a flurry of activity for the altar guild. The brass and silver are polished with exceptional care, the church is immaculately cleaned and very special flowers are planned. White flowers on the altar are traditional, but red is also appropriate for such occasions. When the bishop's chair is placed outside the altar rail, the addition of a nearby pedestal of flowers accentuates the import of his presence. A dramatic and appropriate design, simulating the flame of the Holy Spirit, consists of red gladioli and carnations at the bottom, melding into orange gladioli and tangerine carnations, with yellow gladioli forming the tip of the fiery tongue.

There are many other special services besides those we have mentioned. Each requires specific, imaginative and lovingly created flower arrangements. These special services mark momentous occasions in the life of a church and its congregation. The duties of the altar guild include the privilege, as well as the responsibility of translating the common emotion, inherent in each event, into floral arrangements worthy of these occasions.

X

CHRISTMAS

As Christmas approaches with the hubbub of cooking, shopping, wrapping and parties, one sometimes feels the world has forgotten the Christian meaning of this feast. The members of the Washington Cathedral Altar Guild believe that through the beauty of wreaths, garlands, trees and special flower arrangements we are visually reminding all who come to the cathedral that the birthday of our Savior is both a solemn and joyous occasion.

Just as many individual families enjoy decorating their homes for the holiday season, so the church family often comes together to decorate God's house. After the service on the fourth Sunday of Advent, and prior to Christmas Eve, many churches hold a Hanging of the Greens service and party which happily involves the entire congregation. Each member enjoys his assigment, whether decorating window sills, roping the balcony with evergreen swags, afixing potted plants to the rood screen or wreathing the front door. Even the children wish to be included by decorating a small tree with ornaments they have made.

Numerous areas in and about the church lend themselves to special treatment. Among these are:

1) The front door—wreaths—evergreen/Della Robia
   a) An evergreen wreath can be made of local material such as spruce, cedar or boxwood either on a wreath form covered with sphagnum moss or simply on a coat hanger bent into a circle with the greens attached in sections with florist wire.
   b) Make a Della Robia wreath by covering a wreath form with thoroughly soaked sphagnum moss. This should not be the shredded garden variety. Secure it onto the form by criss-crossing heavy dark thread or fishing line all the way around. Remove the leaves

from previously conditioned branches of camellia or laurel for small wreaths, or magnolia for large wreaths. Put three leaves together and fan them out so that when the two end leaves are curved around they will cover the frame sides. Place the cluster onto the moss and secure it with a florist pin stuck through the base. Make another cluster and place it in shingle-laying fashion to overlap the base of the previous cluster. Continue this process all the way around. When the wreath is completely covered, wrap it tightly with wet cloth strips, being careful that the side leaves are molded to the contour of the covered frame. Let the wrapped wreath sit overnight in a cool place. When the strips are removed the leaves will remain molded. Using treated fruits (See Chapter XII.) in scale with the size of the wreath, arrange them in four separate points with florist pins and/or florist picks. In the remaining four sections of leaves criss-cross blue ribbon. This may be purchased weather-proofed for outside doors or velvet for indoors.

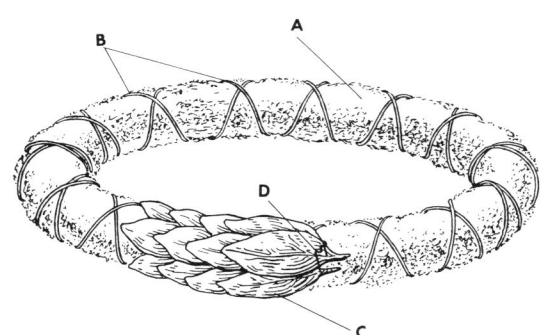

A Della Robia wreath is constructed by covering a wire wreath form into soaked sphagnum moss (A) which is secured by criss-crossing fishing line (B). The conditioned leaves are placed in groups of three (C) in shingle fashion anchored by florist pins (D).

2) The Narthex
    a) This is a perfect, cool spot for a living Christmas tree which could be planted later in the church yard.
    b) The notice board or tract rack may need sprucing up. To treat either of these locations a small piece of soaked oasis is completely wrapped in green florist foil. Tape it with adhesive tape to the wood, and cover it completely by inserting sprigs of pine and holly. Brighten it with the addition of red miniature carnations.

3) The Font
   a) The previously mentioned children's tree decorated with their ornaments is most appropriate.
   b) If the minister or rector has no objection, the font makes an ideal pedestal to hold a dishpan beehive for flowers.
4) Windows
   a) Many churches celebrate midnight services by candlelight. Window sills are an effective location for candles set in logs or oasis and surrounded by greens and holly berries. The greens must be very fresh and the candles long enough to last throughout the service without burning down to the greens. Nothing is less conducive to worship than having one ear on "The Word" and one eye on the low-burning candles. Followers are a great help in controlling the burning of the candles.
5) The lectern/pulpit area
   a) Design a single pedestal arrangement to be placed in front of the lectern from which the Christmas story will be read, or in front of the pulpit where the minister will deliver his Christmas message.
   b) Matching box arrangements on each end of the step or steps leading from the nave floor to the sanctuary give a festive frame to the chancel and the altar.

Other parts of the church may be decorated, but the total effect should be one of joyful restraint and good taste. Never overshadow the focal point of the service which is the table of our Lord. The flower committee should design and execute the most imaginative and beautiful arrangement to point up the cross and its meaning of the gift of love and sacrifice.

In the eyes of many, decorating for Christmas is almost synonymous with evergreens, holly and poinsettias. In years past, flower arrangers struggled with cut poinsettias by burning the stems, conditioning them, and arranging the blossoms, then prayed that these capricious cut flowers would not droop by midnight. The relaxing of certain rigid restrictions, such as using potted material on the retable, has solved the arranger's dilemma. The Washington Cathedral policy states that *any natural material,* fresh, dried or potted, lovingly and artistically arranged for the glory of God is acceptable.

With this new freedom, therefore, and with the hardy new varieties of poinsettias now available, including pink, white and variegated hybrids, poinsettias are handled with versatility and confidence. The Washington

Cathedral Altar Guild uses a procedure of preparing small individual plants so that they can be treated as cut blossoms. In September the team members responsible for Christmas decorations decide on the design they wish to execute and estimate the number and color of blossoms they will require. We then call the supplier and give him our order, specifying that the plants be no taller than six inches and there be no more than three plants to an eight-inch pot. More than three to a pot cannot be successfully separated without plant loss, as the roots are too entwined. The pots are delivered several days prior to arranging. To process them, we set up a production line of at least three people. The first person soaks each pot in a large pan deep enough to submerge the entire flower pot. When the air has stopped bubbling up from the soil, the pot is lifted to a drain tray. After the pot is drained, the second person tilts it to dislodge the dirt by pushing a finger through the hole in the bottom. The plants then are gently separated, keeping some soil around each root structure. The excess dirt is saved for the church garden. For each plant the third person opens a pint freezer bag, inserts the roots and dirt, squeezes out all the air and carefully, but firmly, secures a twistem around the stem of the bagged plant. Treated in this fashion the plants may be handled as individual blossoms and will last about ten days without watering. If one should wilt it is easy to open its bag and add a small amount of water. Be very sparing in doing this as too much water causes the green leaves to turn yellow and drop.

While bagged poinsettias can be used in arrangements in vases and compotes, the number of blossoms in the design is limited because of the bagged root mass. If you are planning a larger festive arrangement, we recommend the use of boxes or frames.

Boxes are ideal containers when constructing large Christmas arrangements whose background is usually of evergreens, particularly the conifers. These long, thick branches require the bracing and base support best afforded by such containers. Background evergreens will remain fresh the twelve days of Christmas if they are positioned in boxes containing pinholders and chicken wire or oasis and watered every few days. (For mechanics see Chapter VI—Boxes, and Chapter VIII—Foliage.) This is particularly important for altar guilds such as ours which keep the decorations in place throughout the Christmas season.

When Christmas falls early in the week consider arranging the festival green background as the altar decoration for the fourth Sunday in Advent. By so doing the arranger can spend more time on this, and need only return on Christmas Eve to transform the semi-penitential greens into the planned glorious festival arrangement by placing poinsettias into the design. The bagged poinsettias may be added "face on" or in profile, making certain that the plastic bagged roots are completely hidden among the greens. Often small pieces of styrofoam placed on the retable, or braced among the greens will help support the stem of "face on" poinsettias. For higher blossom placement, a plant may be fastened to a bamboo stake by carefully cradling the bagged roots with twistem and securing it to the stake. This method is advisable since merely attaching the plant stem to the stake may cause the brittle stem to snap due to the weight below.

In box arrangements the altar guild also has the option of combining poinsettias with cut flowers. For those churches where only white flowers are permitted for Christmas, consider using the soft spike lines of white snapdragons with the white poinsettias. To achieve greater interest, add a few white Majestic daisies for contrast in shape and concentration of brilliant white. To give more emphasis to the dimension of the design, add a few yellow pompom chrysanthemums well back into the mechanics. This still will have the appearance of an all-white arrangement but it gives the illusion of sun shining through the flowers. In churches where the use of color is not prohibited, many striking arrangements may be designed by combining unusual shades. For example, if you are planning a red motif, a clear red color gladioli, such as Valerian, mixed with red poinsettias is electrified by the introduction of tangerine carnations. When your color scheme is pink instead of traditional red, the effect becomes more vivid if dark red and pink snapdragons and hot pink carnations are added to the pink poinsettias. Altar guilds often overlook pink as the color for their Christmas designs, but we recommend its consideration for an innovative change.

Christmas altar decorations arranged upon frames are unique and dramatic. They are unique because they are unparalleled for mass use of color. They are dramatic because of their stylized form. (See Appendix How to Build a Frame.)

To execute this kind of arrangement begin by attaching bits of well-conditioned green to floral picks and threading the picks through the chicken wire. This forms the green outline. Now the poinsettias may be positioned. Always start at the top of the frame and work down. Cradle the bagged roots and dirt with a piece of twistem leaving the two ends long enough to go

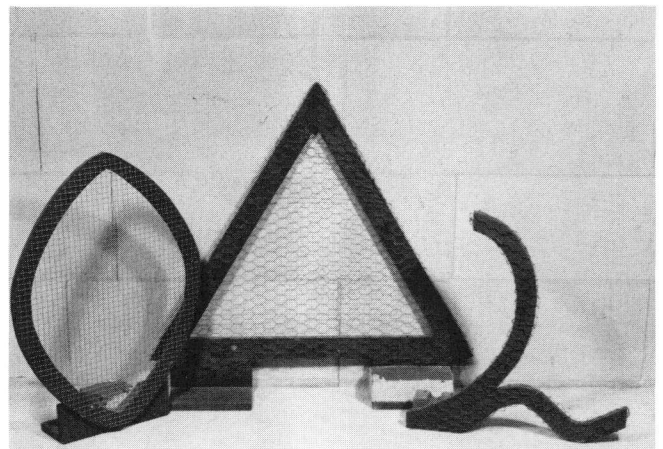

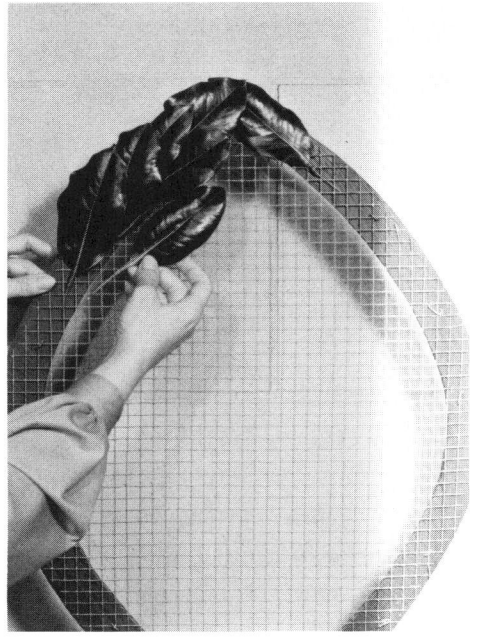

through to the back where they are tightly twisted around the chicken wire. Overlap each succeeding plant so that its blossom will cover the bag of the plant above. This will present a mass display of color. The bagged roots of the bottom line are covered by greens which serve to hide the bags as well as join the arrangement to the retable. If the arranger desires to emphasize individual blossoms, the bags of each plant are secured to the chicken wire and covered by greens.

The time, effort, talent, and love spent to arrange the flowers for Christmas are our gift to God on the anniversary of His Son's birth. May this gift always be worthy of his gift of love, sacrifice and peace to all men of good will. Gloria in excelsis Deo!

XI

EASTER

Easter is the most joyous and holy day in the church calendar. This glorious festival presents the members of the altar guild with the greatest challenge of the entire year. Within a few hours the church must be transformed from the starkness of Good Friday to the glory of Easter.

Varying dates of Easter, which fall between March 23rd and April 24th, further challenge the flower committee since flowers that are available one year may have come and gone in another year. This need not be an obstacle. Indeed, it may be an advantage because different materials are available to make diverse designs in successive years.

Easter lilies, which symbolize Easter for most of us, are normally found in profusion as growers schedule their planting for blossoms during Eastertide. Whether they are purchased as potted plants or cut flowers, lilies are surprisingly economical for the Easter display. Most stems contain several blossoms in various stages from bud to fully matured blooms. Lily buds continue to open into new blooms so an arrangement will remain fresh and can be held over successfully for a second week.

As Easter lilies are used in most churches, it is important to know what extra steps should be observed in addition to those usually followed in proper conditioning of flowers. The anthers of each blossom must be *carefully* removed as the pollen stains the fair linen. We stress the word carefully for, if the anthers are removed without touching the pistil, the flowers remain unfertilized and will live longer. This is true for both cut and potted lilies. All buds must be watched so as they open, their anthers are removed. If some of the more mature buds are needed as open flowers, the blooming process can be hurried by cautiously using a fingernail to separate petals. Lift each petal away slightly from the adjoining petals, remove the anthers, and then gently mist the bud with warm water. When the stems of cut lilies are so large that they create problems in arranging them in either chicken wire or beehives they may be successfully pared down with a vegetable peeler. Unfortunately, potted lilies cannot be separated and bagged as poinsettias may be treated, but whole pots of lilies may be used, supplemented by cut lilies, to arrange a magnificent display. These plants grow with their trumpets facing in all directions, so prune the blossoms from the back of the stalk and use them in water picks in the front of the design. Lilies have now been bred to eliminate the heavy scent, a boon to many who found the odor overpowering. It seems a pity to remove all the sweet perfume of spring. However, by incorporating delicate freesia or a few hyacinths somewhere in the church, a touch of fragrance is restored.

Stately arrangements, as well as lavish altar displays, can be made solely of Easter lilies artfully styled against handsome green backgrounds. Other lovely altar arrangements can be created with lilies in conjunction with various flowers. If Easter falls when flowering shrubs, fruit trees or dogwood are in bloom, the addition of these materials will add grace to the angular line of lilies. Dogwood should not be cut in the woods, but garden trees do need pruning. White snapdragons and gladioli, in combination with both potted and cut lilies, make a glorious pair of box arrangements for the altar.

If your church is not bound to the tradition of using all white flowers for Easter, consider some of the lovely colorations of spring, particularly those of the other bulbs. Varying shades of yellow of tulips, jonquils and narcissus give the feeling of new life. The tones of the sunrise also are an inspiration for a new and unusual design.

At Washington Cathedral the first Eucharist of the day is celebrated in Resurrection Chapel. There, in the area above the altar, the Easter message of the sunrise and the risen Christ is executed in mosaic. This sunrise became the inspiration for box arrangements which, when completed, reproduced the rising sun theme in flowers. Sometimes this design is carried out all over the cathedral. Even in those when other altars are decked with different arrangements we always have at least one sunrise arrangement. One year this design might be done with a flaming orange sun of mid-century lilies with emanating rays of yellow and white snapdragons. Another year the arrangement is highly shaded with the red of anthurium for the sun, radiating to pink, and finally to white with spikes of snapdragons or gladioli.

60

To construct a sunrise, set up a pair of boxes with extra supporting mechanics, as described in Chapter VI. These are right-angled triangles which will be placed close to the cross. The greens consist of ti or aspidistra leaves which reinforce the feeling of rays. When the background is in place begin the outline of flowers with two bunches of white snapdragons. The inner rays, consisting of two bunches of yellow snapdragons, are placed, and finally four stems of mid-century lilies, two at each inside corner of the boxes, are inserted for the sun. For stronger color the flower order is changed to one bunch of yellow snapdragon and one bunch of yellow Dutch iris which will outline the orange sun in a more vivid yellow. A smaller green-leafed material is used to join the flowers to the containers and hide the rim of the boxes.

In addition to the arrangements which adorn the cross and altar, two other areas of the church may need special attention for Holy Saturday services. They are the site of the paschal candle where the new fire will be lighted, and the baptistry or font area if there are to be baptisms.

If the pavement candlestick holding the paschal candle is ornate, use a very simple design for the arrangement. A test tube secured with floral tape containing a single lily stem and a bit of camouflaging green is sufficient. If the candlestick is plain, the flower committee may choose to enhance it with a garland of greens and flowers, or a small "garden" at its base.

The steps to construct and attach the garland are quite simple. Place on a cutting board a block of soaked and drained oasis with its perforated side as the front. Cut it in half down the length of the block. While holding the two pieces together, turn them one quarter turn so the perforations are now on the top and slice them into six equal parts. This gives twelve oasis segments approximately 1½ inch square by 4½ inches long which is the correct size to fit into a quart freezer bag leaving enough plastic at each end to wrap a twistem tightly around it. Repeat this process until you have enough completed bag segments to make a rope which will wind down the length of the paschal candlestick. Begin making the rope by joining the bottom end of one bag to the top of another with wire wrapped three or four times around the overlapping ends. Use wire on a spool so that you can have one continuous length of wire joining all the bags. Overlap the bottom end of the third bag to the top of the second and tightly wrap the wire around these ends. Continue this procedure until all are joined. The rope looks like link sausages with a wire running the full length of it. Remember which end of the garland has the last attached segment because this end must be the top of

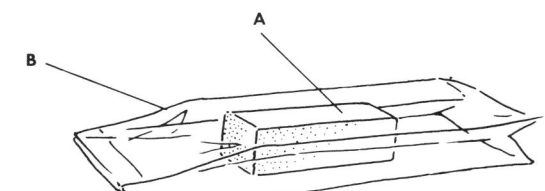

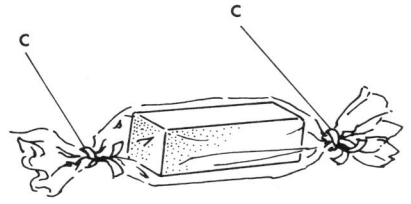

To construct garlands one twelfth of a block of oasis (A) is inserted into a quart freezer bag (B) and each end is secured by twistem (C). One continuous length of No. 28 spool wire (D) is wrapped at each segment.

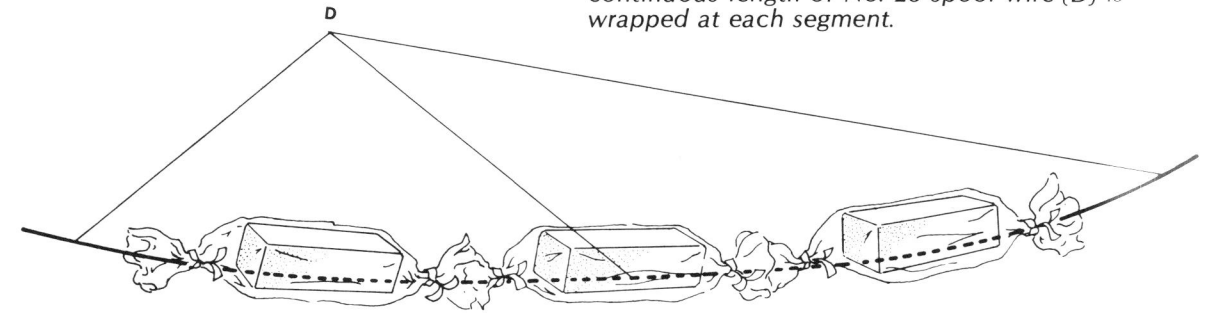

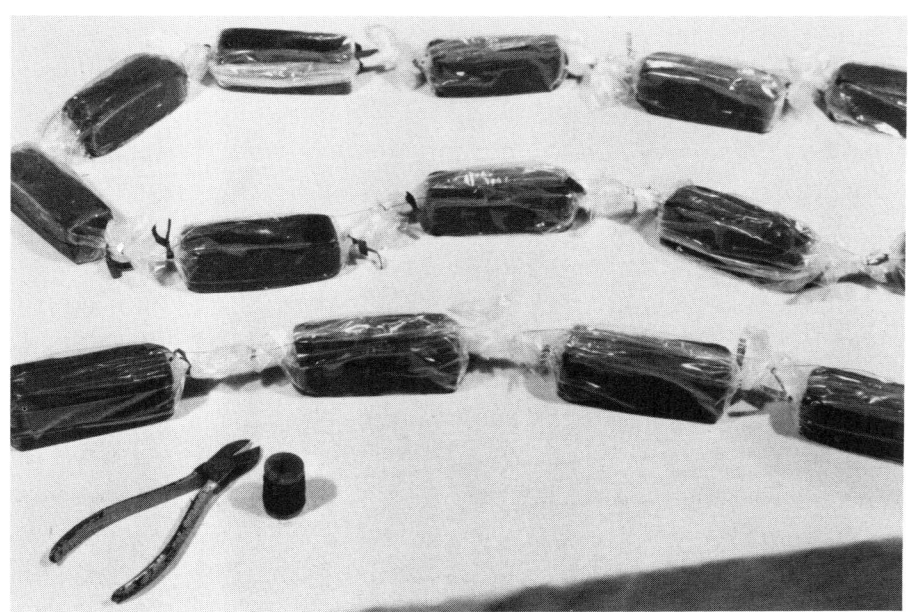

the garland. If the process is followed as outlined water won't leak out of any of the bags once the arrangement has been set in place. For ease in placing the material, stick in all the green background around all three sides while the garland is lying flat on the working surface. Then follow with the flower placement. We suggest long lasting and sturdy-stemmed flowers such as white starburst chrysanthemums, white statice and baby's breath. These will remain fresh through the first Sunday after Easter if the garland is misted several times during the week. Although attaching the decoration is not difficult, it can be tricky, so we recommend that two persons work together. Construct a sturdy anchor of wire, securely wrapped around the candlestick, below the bobeche. Floral tape also may be used for added security. Wire the free end of the top of the rope to this anchor. Carefully place the back side of this top segment against the candlestick and continue carefully winding the rope down the shaft. At the base of the candlestick hold the last segment firmly in place and, with a piece of wire long enough to go around the base several times, attach the wire to the bag end. Complete by wrapping the wire around the base and pinching it firmly to lock the end of the garland in place. Next, step back and study the arrangement. You probably will find places that need additional flowers. The finishing touch comes with placing greens at the top and bottom of the garland to hide the attaching mechanics. Garlands are also effective when used to decorate columns, the pulpit, the lectern, the font, a rood screen, a balcony or any appropriate area in the church. If the area selected requires a long garland, it is advisable to secure the mechanics first and then insert the greens and flowers.

One of the loveliest and most unusual Easter decorations is a spring garden growing inside the church. It is equally charming done very simply or on a more lavish scale. Plan a small garden in the font area, in a corner, or in the space usually used for the Christmas crèche. In any event, situate it where it can be seen, but will not obstruct the procession or ritual of your church. Lay a piece of plastic, the size of the garden you wish to construct, down on the floor. Position window boxes or bread pans filled with small pots of annual plants such as geranium, alyssum, pansies, petunias or impatiens interspersed with trailing ivy to mask the boxes. Add several pots of hyacinths grouped with matching shades of hydrangeas. For a sweet-smelling, all-white garden, the altar guild might consider a Lenten project of each member raising one bowl of paper narcissus planted on Ash Wednesday and all returned together on Holy Saturday for the Easter garden. After the plant-filled containers are arranged to achieve their best effect, cover them and the exposed plastic with moss from the woods, or any of a number of garden mulch materials such as wood chips, shredded bark or sphagnum moss. If your church has a spacious vestibule, or an area inside the church where a larger garden may be placed, follow the same directions as above, but use additional mechanics and materials. Purchase a small tree or flowering shrub which will be planted later in the church garden. Keep the dirt ball in the burlap bag, and place it on the plastic. Surround it with steps made of bricks or concrete blocks. Flank the dirt ball with potted plants on the step levels. Add a container nearby in which a clump of pussy willows or flowering branches are arranged to look like a growing plant. Camouflage all mechanics with fern plants or ivy. Complete the garden by enclosing it with end-to-end pieces of logs. On Easter Monday these plants could be distributed to the ill or elderly in lieu of dismantling the altar arrangement which could last through the week and be refurbished for the first Sunday after Easter.

These suggestions are by no means meant to be limiting. Study your church for locations to decorate with a small container filled with flowers. Do you have a table at the rear of the church for service leaflets? Are there steps to a rood screen? Is there a top ledge of a screen dividing a chapel from the nave? If no baptisms are scheduled, and if you have the permission of your minister, consider using the font as a pedestal for a lovely, loose arrangement of flowers and branches. In any event, the entire Easter display throughout the church should be as beautiful as the flower committee can devise.

The arrival of spring with its new growth and bursting forth of flowers proclaims "He is risen!" With joy and love the altar guild cleans, polishes and decorates the church to affirm corporately their Christian faith. "The Lord is risen indeed. Alleluia!"

XII

THANKSGIVING

Thankfulness for the harvest bounty may be expressed by a variety of media. Traditionally, one thinks of the yield of the harvest primarily in terms of fruit, vegetables, wheat and corn. However, this limits the possibilities for many interesting arrangements that may be designed from year to year. Indeed, fruits and vegetables denote the harvest season and should be used, but there are other products of God's creation available in the fall season which are equally appropriate for use, either by themselves, or in various combinations with produce. Besides the traditional designs of fruits and vegetables, an arrangement of chrysanthemums connotes the autumn season. A motif consisting of a variety of differently shaped breads arranged with wheat and grapes also signifies the harvest bounty.

Our choice of media is determined by the date of Thanksgiving in relation to the first Sunday in Advent. While Thanksgiving is always celebrated on the fourth Thursday in November, Advent is a movable feast. Depending upon the year, the first Sunday in Advent may, or may not, fall on the Sunday directly following Thanksgiving. For economy of time and budget, our Thanksgiving arrangements always serve as the decor, not only for the Thanksgiving festival itself, but also for one Sunday. If the first Sunday in Advent falls immediately after Thanksgiving, as is usually the case, our arrangements are set in place on the Saturday before Thanksgiving to remain the seven days of Saturday through Friday. Then we dismantle the harvest decorations and arrange only evergreens for the semi-penitential season of Advent. Those few years when Advent does not begin the Sunday following Thanksgiving, the festival arrangements are done on the Wednesday before the holiday and held over for five days through the following weekend. The designs and materials we choose depend upon how long the arrangements must last, whether it be one week or five days.

With the careful selection of materials and proper treatment of them, the arrangements can last a full ten days if they are to last from the Saturday through Thanksgiving to the following Sunday. These are started on the Saturday prior to Thanksgiving, fresh flowers added on Wednesday, and then held over through the second weekend. Any one of these timetables extends the spirit of the harvest season, allows greater appreciation of the festival arrangements and conserves altar flower funds.

After determing the length of time the Thanksgiving arrangements will be in place, the choice of materials is decided. Here is a partial list of possibilities from least perishable to most perishable:

DRIED MATERIALS		
	bittersweet	milkweed pods
	bread and rolls	okra pods
	cat tails	sea oats (endangered species, use only commercially grown)
	celosia	
	corn shocks	straw flowers
	glycerinized leaves (eucalyptus, magnolia, ti)	teasel
		wheat
	goldenrod	yarrow
	Indian corn	

TREATABLE MATERIALS		
	apples	oranges
	artichokes	persimmons*
	bananas*	pineapples*
	gourds	pomegranates*
	grapefruit*	pumpkins*
	grapes*	squash (crooknecked, acorn, hubbard, turban)
	kumquats*	*may decay sooner.
	lady apples	
	lemons	

MOST PERISHABLE MATERIALS	fresh flowers, with the exception of stripped chrysanthemums, unshellacked fruits and vegetables

66

Why do we treat the edible materials? The main reason is to retard spoilage, but this also discourages fruit flies and the darting fingers of little choir members. Can the fruits and vegetables be used after treating? Items which can be peeled are edible. However, when a parish church chooses to prolong a Thanksgiving arrangement by preserving the fruits and vegetables, the savings can be used to purchase a food basket for the needy.

To preserve the produce, all fruits and vegetables, with the exception of grapes, are shellacked prior to arranging. This is done with clear shellac and brushes. A single carefully applied coat over the entire surface is sufficient. Certain fruits and vegetables, notably green peppers, apples and cucumbers, and sometimes citrus fruits, are treated with a wax preservative by the growers before shipping. Shellac will not adhere to these surfaces. When using these materials try to obtain them from a local farmer, or remove the coating with a mild solvent. We do not recommend spray shellac because (1) it is wasteful, (2) one cannot be sure that the object will be completely sealed, and (3) most importantly, the propellant agent tends to discolor some fruits, especially bananas. If any cut fruits are used such as half lemon or orange, or part of a pineapple, they should be shellacked on the outside in the usual manner. After drying, they are cut and left to callus overnight. The cut surface is then thoroughly sprayed with a product such as Floralife's Superior Surface Sealer. In experimenting, one half lemon lasted a month treated in this fashion. Grapes are shellacked in place after the arrangement is complete. If they are done ahead of time the bunches would not fall gracefully in position.

Having chosen the materials to arrange, the next step is to select the design and the mechanics for it. The following designs are suggested with the use of materials from the least to the most perishable.

1) DRIED MATERIALS ON FRAMES (for constructing frames see Appendix 3)

If the reredos is light stone, or is a light colored dossal, the frames are edged in greenery. Choose a long-lasting kind, such as magnolia or arbor-vitae, which will not shed, fade or curl out of water. Either thread the stems into the chicken wire or attach the leaves to wooden floral picks and thread the picks completely around the wire edge. With the green outline in place, begin fastening the flower material at the top of the framework and work down to the base. Meld the colors from cream through yellow, orange, red to bronze so that the weight is at the bottom. This creates a dramatic design of fall colors which will last for at least ten days.

2) SYMBOLS OF THE EUCHARIST

In advance of Thanksgiving obtain pairs of leftover French rolls, as well as loaves of French, wheat, white, pumpernickle and braided Challah breads. The bread needs no further preserving treatment other than that of drying out. We have found no evidence of nibblings, so either we have no church mouse or he is unable to climb up onto the retables.

First place strips of plastic on the retable. Fill a pair of boxes with styrofoam which protrudes about two inches above the rims, and place the containers on the plastic. Behind the extreme ends of the boxes set a pair of No. 7 pinholders on the plastic. For the outside vertical line, thrust into these pinholders branches of magnolia or other greens which will survive out of water. Arrange a handful of graduating lengths of wheat, and secure the bunch with twistem. Add this to the pinholder. Then begin the arrangement of bread with the loaf of French bread. Push one end of a bamboo stake into the loaf and the other end into the styrofoam, so that the long diagonal line appears to link the magnolia and wheat to the box. Add the other loaves at different attitudes to produce a descending line ending with the French roll. To tie the design together and complete the line, add more magnolia and wheat horizontally into the styrofoam. An optional touch which will spark the arrangement is the addition of several lemons on each side. Finally, with the aid of florist pins, place two or three bunches of green grapes among the loaves. When you are satisfied with the design, shellac the grapes. If any bunches hang over the sides slip a paper towel or piece of plastic underneath them to catch any shellac which might drip onto the altar, retable or the container.

3. TREATED FRUITS AND VEGETABLES

Many different designs are available, using properly treated produce, as the arranger has imagination to create. The following few illustrations are helpful to show how some of these are constructed.

(a) ON FRAMES: Before attaching any other materials, remember to fill in the green outside line if the background is light. There are two easy ways to use floral picks with fruits and vegetables so that they can be securely fastened into the frame. One method is to stick a pick directly into each piece so that the wire on the other end of the pick is free. Position the piece by holding it in one hand, and with the other hand wrap the pick to the chicken wire. The second method uses the floral pick in a different way. Twist the wire of the pick to the stem of the piece of fruit, and simply weave the pick into the chicken wire at the desired position. Start attaching the materials of the lightest color and smallest size at the top, then move down the frame, fastening progressively larger pieces of stronger colors until the largest, deepest colored materials form the base. For added dimension and emphasis of color, occasionally clump several of the same fruits and vegetables together at various intervals. To link the base of the arrangement to the retable fill in a good bottom line with greens.

(b) CONES IN VASES AND COMPOTES: Secure a pinholder to the bottom of the container with a generous amount of floral clay. Press a styrofoam cone as deeply as possible into the pinholder. For stability, slowly push a bamboo stake down at a sharp angle from the back of the cone into the pinholder. This is used in addition to attaching

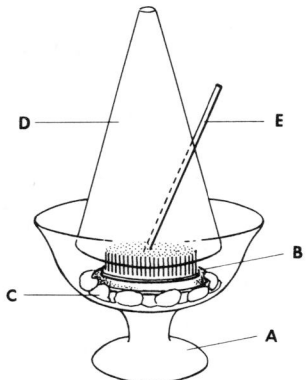

Mechanics for a styrofoam cone consist of a footed compote (A) with a pinholder (B) secured by a generous amount of floral clay (C). The cone (D) is impaled on the pinholder and reinforced by a bamboo stake (E) driven at a sharp angle through the cone into the pinholder (B).

weights to the back rim of the container to counterbalance heavy materials of the design on the front of the cone. Begin by securing fruits and vegetables to the styrofoam with floral pins. For heavier materials two pins may be needed at different angles to insure rigidity.

In securing unusually shaped material, such as gourds, and crooknecked squash, more than two pins may be required, particularly if a specific top-heavy angle of the material is desired. Since this design is a matched pair, one should proceed in coordinate steps as outlined in Chapter IV. One of our team captains reported that her produce man thought her strange when she lined up a bin of crooknecked squash to choose matched pairs. When he found out why she was going through this peculiar exercise he enthusiastically opened other crates of squash so that together they could find seven matched pairs of varying sizes. For color-carrying power and dimension some materials may be grouped. To achieve this effect, secure several pieces to the cone. Pierce the other pieces with florist pins so the prongs stick out of the back. Then attach them onto the already placed fruit. Another three dimensional effect is created by impaling the fruit on a bamboo garden stake which previously has been thrust into the cone. After all the rest of the fruit is in place decide upon the position of the bunches of grapes. Insert a florist pick into the cone at the point where the top of the bunch is to be located. Weave a portion of the thin wire of the exposed pick end through the top of the bunch, and wrap the remainder securely around the pick. Move the grapes to the desired angle, hold the bunch in one hand, straddle a florist pin over the stem near the base, and push the pin into the cone. When the arrangement is complete the grapes are shellacked with great care to protect the container, retable and altar area.

(c) FIRESIDE WICKER BASKETS: These make handsome containers for the fruits of the harvest. Grasp the handle and tilt the basket forward to the desired open angle for display. Secure a No. 7 pinholder with florist wire to the underneath side at the place which is now the bottom of the container. Carve a piece of styrofoam to fit inside the basket and wire it in several places. With a piece of plastic on the retable, position the basket with the handle and styrofoam facing out. Be sure to angle the baskets so that the handles are not viewed straight on but appear curved.Now arrange the fruits and vegetables, attaching them to the styrofoam with picks, pins and bamboo stakes allowing some to spill out gracefully onto the plastic covering on the retable.

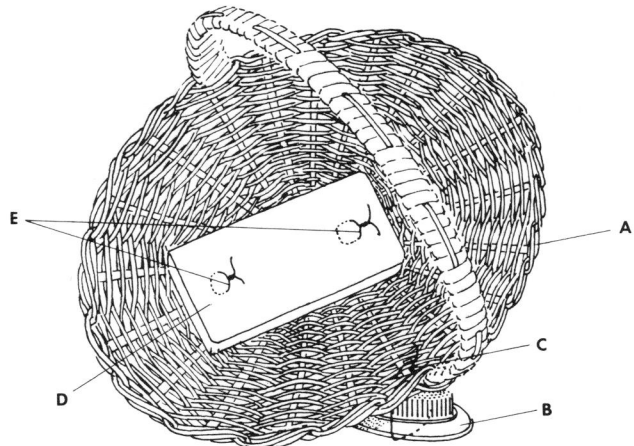

A fireside basket (A) has a #7 pinholder (B) wired (C) to the underside of the basket, after a styrofoam block (D) has been wired (E) to the bottom center.

(d) FORMS WITHOUT CONTAINERS: Carve a square sheet of styrofoam into a trapezoid by cutting a triangle from each side. Place this form onto a second square sheet as a pattern to carve the other trapezoid. Force each form vertically into the front of a No. 7 pinholder. For security push a bamboo stake from the middle area of the front at a downward angle through the styrofoam into the pinholder. Position

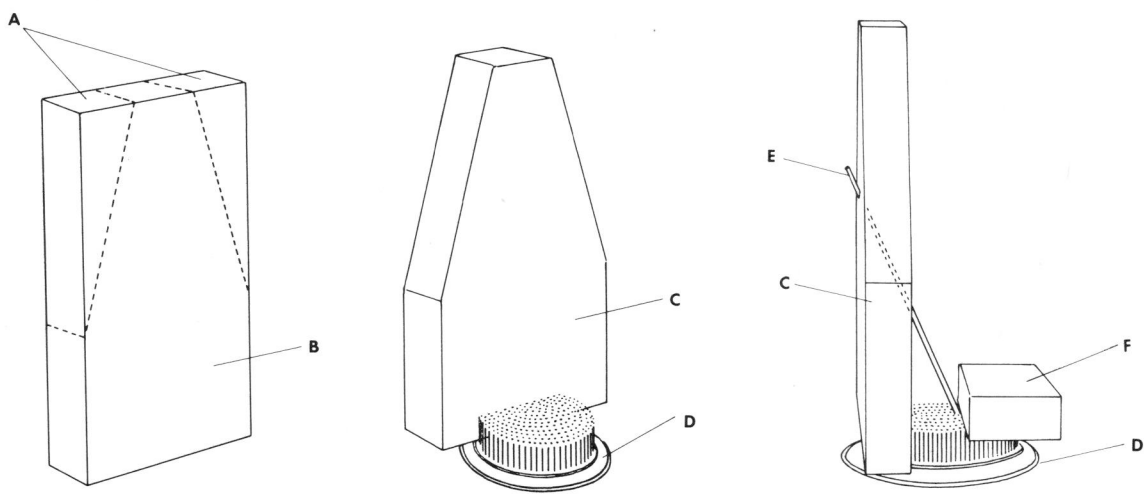

To create a trapezoid slice a pair of triangles (A) from a 20" x 9" x 2" sheet of styrofoam (B). Force the trapezoid (C) into the front of a #7 pinholder (D). For support thrust a bamboo stake (E) at an acute angle into the pinholder. Counterbalance with at least one brick (F).

71

the pair where they are to remain, as the design is executed in place. Force a bamboo stake vertically into the center of the top, leaving enough of the stake above to support a whole or a half pineapple impaled upon it. As the weight force is straight down, there is no fear of the styrofoam tearing away from the pinholder. Proceed by adding smaller fruits and vegetables, such as lady apples, lemons and grapes with floral picks and pins, leaving the larger materials to lie directly on the retable forming the base of the design. Soften the harsh side lines with bits of green. For greens that will not hold up out of water, put them in water picks before inserting them into the design. Bricks or lead puddles are periodically added on the back of the pinholder to counterbalance the growing weight of the front.

4. FLOWERS COMBINED WITH TREATED FRUITS AND VEGETABLES

Many decorative arrangements result from combining fresh flowers with fruits and vegetables. Since the flowers are more perishable than the treated materials, select a hearty type and arrange them with long lasting background and cover greens in a pair of boxes with pinholders and chicken wire mechanics. (See Chapter VIII.) Large disbud chrysanthemums, such as Peter Johns or Red Rovers, are long lived and particularly striking when coordinated with the color of fruits and vegetables. Strip off all the stem greens of the chrysanthemums as these will wither and brown in a few days. Done in this manner the flower portion of the design will remain fresh for about a week. Now complete the arrangement by adding treated fruits and vegetables in front to hide the boxes, allowing them to taper outward in size from pumpkins to lemons across the plastic covered retable. The end result is a burst of flowers arising out of an arc of brightly colored fruits and vegetables.

We exhort you to shellac pumpkins thoroughly. One Thanksgiving we had a catastrophe on the high altar of Washington Cathedral. The guild members performing the shellacking duties the week prior to Thanksgiving decided the huge pumpkins designated for the High Altar looked firm and fresh enough to forego treatment. On the Saturday before Thanksgiving the arranging took place, and each of the altars was spectacular. The Sunday worshippers and tourists pronounced the decor a success. On Thursday, Thanksgiving Day, in the middle of the service of Holy Communion, with the bishop celebrating, there was a mighty WHOooosh! The right hand pumpkin heaved, collapsed inward, and a great cloud of fruit flies sallied forth. Before the service could continue the verger had to scurry to the Sacristy, produce a can of disinfectant, and spray the unwelcome visitors. No item has gone untreated since!

5. UNTREATED FRUITS AND VEGETABLES

Many untreated materials will last only a short time in a heated church. If the purpose is to keep them in their natural state for distribution to the sick and needy, do not use most of the mechanics described above. Florist picks or bamboo stakes will cause green holes, and florist pins leave metal prick holes which render these items inappropriate to be given. The fruits are edible, but they should be given only to those who would not be offended by receiving damaged goods. Our altar guild members help return a portion of the cost of Thanksgiving decorations by purchasing at a reduced price those items that are still partially usable.

At no other season of the year are so many different kinds of materials available at one time to join in unlimited combinations for the creation of truly ingenious and wonderfully meaningful designs. Begin thinking of your Thanksgiving decor in September or early October as the time of harvest approaches. Take a new look at shapes and colors in the market. Dream up designs unique to your church. Then in November execute your arrangement, and return to church on Thanksgiving Day with a heart filled with praise and thanks.

APPENDIX 1

Amaryllis	Cut in water.
*Anemone	Cut in water. When they begin to droop dip stem ends in alcohol for a few seconds or rub with salt.
Anthurium	Cut in water.
Asparagus fern	Use boiling water method.
*Aster	Cut in water. (1) If they begin to droop crush stem ends, then use boiling water or burning method. (2) Dip in peppermint oil or alcohol for a few seconds.
Azalea	Cut in water.
Bamboo	Use vinegar method on smaller stemmed bamboo. After the larger bamboo has been cut it will not draw water. To preserve it pierce holes down through the center to the bottom node, or drill a small hole through the side just below each node and fill the stem with water.
Bellflower	Cut in water. If they start to droop use burning method.
Bird-of-Paradise (Strelitzia)	Cut in water.
Bittersweet	Cut in water. If it is to be dried, spray with clear lacquer.
Black-eyed Susan	Cut in water. If they begin to droop, recut and use boiling water method.
Calendula	Cut in water.
Calla Lily	Cut in water, Rub stem ends with salt, let stand a few minutes, then recut in water.
Camellia	Cut in water. Press dressmaker's pin through center of blossom into stem to hold it in place, or apply damp salt to the base of the stamens with a match or toothpick.
Candytuft	Cut in water. If they start to droop, use the boiling water method.
Carnation	Cut in water.
Cherry Blossom	Split stem ends and place in a bucket of deep water.
Chrysanthemum	The greatest problem here is to preserve the leaves which usually wilt before the flower. Always sprinkle underside of leaves with water. Cut in water, scrape, split or crush stem ends, or break stems with fingers and use boiling water method then stand in cold water overnight. Can also split cut end, and dip in peppermint oil for a few seconds.

Cockscomb	Cut in water. When the leaves begin to droop use the boiling water method.
Cornflower	Cut in water.
Cosmos	Crush stem ends and rub with salt, use burning method or dip in peppermint oil for a few seconds.
Daffodil	Cut in water.
*Dahlia	Cut in water, use boiling water method or crush cut end slightly and dip in peppermint oil or alcohol for a few seconds.
Delphinium	Cut in water.
Dogwood	Split stem ends, stand in warm water and leave overnight.
*Elaeagnus	Burn cut end, dip in alcohol for two or three seconds.
Evergreens	Split stem ends and stand in deep cold water overnight. You can spray lightly from below with clear lacquer to hold the leaves on the branches longer.
Fern	Cut in water or use boiling water method.
Forsythia	Cut in water or split stem ends.
Freesia	Cut in water.
Funkia (Hosta)	Split stem ends and cut in water or dip in peppermint oil.
Gardenia	Cut in water. Spray foliage and blossoms. Submerge in water before arranging.
Geranium	Use boiling water method, or dip in peppermint oil for 2 or 3 seconds.
*Gerbera	Use boiling water method or dip in alcohol.
Gladioli	Cut in water.
Gypsophilia (baby's breath)	Cut in water.
Heather	Cut in water.
Herbaceous peony	Use burning or boiling water method.
Holly	Split stem ends.
*Hydrangea	Use boiling salted water or burning method, or crush the cut ends then dip in alcohol for a few seconds.
Iris	Cut in water and rub in ash.
Lilac	Cut in water, strip all green, or split stem ends and rub them with salt, or use burning method.
Lily	Cut in water.
Magnolia	Split stem ends or use burning method.
Maple	Select in the early part of the day. Cut the stem immediately under water. Strip the bark from the lower end of the stem with a knife. Use the vinegar

method. Let sit in deep water overnight. In the fall of the year when the material is older and seasoned let it sit overnight in deep water/vinegar solution. (One part vinegar to four parts water)

Marigold	Cut in water.
Nandina	Crush stem ends and, if in flower, salt the water lightly.
*Narcissus	Dip in alcohol for five seconds.
Pampas Grass	Cut in water and use the vinegar method.
Pansy	Cut in water.
Paulownia	Split stem ends and dip in vinegar for one minute; scrape bottom inch of stem ends deeply, then crush.
Petunia	Cut in water, then crush stem ends.
Plum	Split the cut end into four parts, rub salt into it and then burn. If it has green leaves dip in peppermint oil for a few seconds.
Poinsettia	Cut in water, then use boiling water or burning method.
Poppy	Cut in water and crush stem ends, or use burning method or dip into peppermint oil for four seconds.
Pussy Willow	Split stem ends.
Reed	Use the vinegar method.
Rhododendron	Cut in water or split stem ends.
*Rose	Scrape potion of stem away, cut in water then crush stem ends; or use boiling or burning method; or split the cut end and rub salt into it or dip in alcohol for a few seconds.
*Rose of Sharon	Burn the cut end; or split the cut end into four parts and dip in vinegar or peppermint oil for five or six seconds or dip in alcohol.
Salvia	Split stem ends and use boiling water method.
Snapdragon	Cut in water or use boiling water method.
Spirea	Split stem ends or dip in peppermint oil.
Stock	Cut in water or use boiling water method, or crush the cut end.
Sweet Pea	Cut in water.
Sweet William	Cut in water, crush stem ends, or use boiling water method.
Thistle	Cut in water and rub cut stem ends with salt, or use burning method.
*Tulip	Cut in water, dip in alcohol three or four seconds, or rub salt into cut end. A florist trick is to make a pin hole in the stem just under the blossom. The

	blossom then will not open. Another method to prevent the flower from opening too quickly is to pinch the stem at the base of the flower with the fingers.
Weeping Willow	No treatment needed.
Yarrow	Crush stem ends, rub with salt or use burning method, or dip in peppermint oil for a few seconds.
Zinnia	Cut in water, remove unnecessary foliage. If leaves begin to wilt use boiling water method, or dip in peppermint oil for a few seconds.

*When the term "alcohol" is used that means whiskey, vodka, sake, NOT rubbing or denatured alcohol.

APPENDIX 2

YELLOW-GREEN/GREEN-WHITE

Aucuba japonica, Japanese aucuba, Gold dust tree
Caladium candidum
Dieffenbachia picta, Dumb Cane
Dracaena fragrans Massangeana
Elaeagnus argentea, Silverberry
Elaeagnus pungens Maculata, Silverberry
Euonymus radicans, Wintercreeper
Euphorbia wulfenii, Spurge
Hosta crispula, Funkia
Hosta fortunei, Funkia
Ligustrum ovalifolium aureum, Golden privet
Ilex aquifolium Aureo Marginata, Holly
Ilex aquifolium, Holly, Golden Queen

BLUE-GREEN

Hosta sieboldiana, Funkia
Mahonia japonica, Hollygrape
Ruta graveolens, Rue
Spiraea vanhoutte, Vanhoutte spirea

GRAY-BLUE

Cedrus atlantica glauca, Atlas cedar
Cynara scolymus, Globe artichoke
Dianthus caryophyllus, Carnation
Echinops, Globe thistle

GRAY-GREEN

Elaeagnus angustifolia, Russian olive
Lavandula, Lavender
Papaver orientale, Poppy
Rosmarinus officinalis, Rosemary
Yucca filamentosa, Adams needle

GRAY-SILVER

Artemisia absinthium, Lambrook Silver
Buddleia fallowinana, Butterfly bush
Cineraria maritima, Dusty miller
Santolina, Lavender cotton
Stachys lanata, Lamb's ears

DEEP GREEN

Camellia japonica
Cytisus, Broom
Hedera, Ivy
Helleborus niger, Christmas rose
Hosta plantaginea, Funkia
Ilex aquifolium, English holly
Kalmia latifolia, Mountain laurel
Ligustrum lucidum, Glossy privet
Magnolia grandiflora, Laurel magnolia
Myrtus communis, Myrtle
Osmanthus ilicifolius, Sweet holly
Pachysandra terminalis, Japanese spurge
Pieris japonica, Japanese andromeda
Prunus laurocerasus, Cherry laurel
Rhododendron
Skimmia japonica
Taxus baccata, English yew
Viburnum rhytidophyllum, Leatherleaf
    viburnum

BRIGHT GREEN

Zantedeschia aethiopica, Calla lily

RED

Acer japonicum, Japanese maple
Coleus, Flame nettle
Quercus palustris, Pin oak

PURPLE

Paeonia, Peony
Rhododendron, Azalea

BRONZE

Canna hortensis, Canna lily
Cryptomeria japonica, Japanese cedar
Forsythia intermedia spectabilis, Golden
    Bells
Leucothoe catesbaei, Drooping leucothoe

BROWN

Fagus sylvatica cuprea, Copper beech
Magnolia grandiflora (reverse side of leaf)
    Laurel magnolia

This is only a partial list of plant material grown in Zone VII, but available in several other Zones. Interesting foliage is to be found everywhere.

The florist can provide Aspidistra, Boxwood, Croton, Eucalyptus, Palm, Strelitzia, Ti and other exotic foliage as well as Cedar, Huckleberry, Laurel, Baker fern (Leatherleaf), Rhododendron, and Salal (Lemon Leaf).

APPENDIX 3

SUGGESTIONS ON HOW TO BUILD FRAMES

We have a number of frames which serve as the mechanics for stylized arrangements for festival seasons. Among these are triangular forms, frames which produce an omega-like design, and round and vesica devices used as a background for the cross.

The frames usually are constructed of one-half or three-quarter-inch thick plywood. The area is covered by double layers of one-inch chicken wire stapled to the framework. Depending on the height and weight of the frame, two or three pieces of one-by-three furring strips are cut long enough so that when the end of each piece is secured perpendicularly to the base, the frame will stand firmly on the retable. Attach these pieces with screws, nuts and bolts or angle irons so they can be removed easily for compact storage.

On a quiet morning sit in the front pew of your church and study the architecture of the sanctuary, with particular attention to the reredos. Do you see Norman arches, Gothic lines, or the soaring diagonals of modern design? What stylized geometric outline would most compliment that architecture and enhance the cross? Since it is relatively easy to construct a frame, or a pair of frames, enlist the aid of a parishioner to build your chosen design. Once they have been made, these can be used time and time again with a variety of materials for various festival occasions.

APPENDIX 4

ARRANGING VOCABULARY

BEEHIVE — the mechanics, combining a saucer, oasis and wire hanging plant basket, necessary for ease of handling narrow-necked vases and pedestals (See Chapters V and VII.)

CONDITIONING OR HARDENING — the processes of preparing cut flowers and foliage for use in arrangements (See Chapter III and Appendix 1.)

DISBUDS — Those flowers whose side buds have been removed during the growing season to produce one large central blossom.

FLORIST BUNCH — The quantity of flowers wrapped together for sale, usually ten stems; for chrysanthemums the stems from one plant, or the equivalent of nine to thirteen ounces depending upon the season.

GREENS — Any leafy material or foliage to be used alone or in combination with flowers for arranging.

HOGARTH CURVE — An artistic term used to describe an S-shaped curve which is rotated slightly counter clockwise on its axis.

MECHANICS — Devices or aids, alone or in combination, needed to give support to the materials of an arrangement.

PEDESTALS — A wide variety of standards used to hold beehive mechanics for the creation of free standing arrangements.

ROOT BALL — The imaginary clump of roots in an arrangement from which all the stems must appear to grow.

ROUNDS — Any of the flowers whose blossom, or cluster of blossoms, grows at the end of a stem, such as chrysanthemums, tulips, roses, daisies, etc.

SPIKES — Those flowers whose blossoms grow along the stems creating strong vertical lines, such as gladioli, delphiniums, snapdragons, and bells of Ireland.

TOPPING UP — The addition of water to completely fill a container.

APPENDIX 5

CHURCH VOCABULARY

ALTAR — The holy table traditionally placed at the east end of a church, now often free-standing and sometimes in the midst of the congregation.

ALTAR RAIL — The railing which encloses the sanctuary containing the altar.

BAPTISTRY — The area of a church in which the baptismal font is located.

CHANCEL — That part of the church comprising the sanctuary and choir, often separated from the nave by the rood screen.

CHAPEL — A small church or a separated section of a larger church containing its own altar and often used for intimate service and private prayer.

DOSSAL — A hanging fabric, sometimes velvet or brocade, placed on the wall behind the altar in lieu of a reredos.

EUCHARISTIC CANDLES — The two candles lighted for the service of Holy Communion. These should be placed on the altar unless they are pavement candles at each end of a free-standing altar.

FAIR LINEN — An altar covering of fine linen cloth usually embroidered with five crosses to represent Christ's wounds.

FONT — A basin to hold the water of baptism, usually mounted on a pedestal of stone or wood.

LECTERN — A stand which holds the Bible.

LITURGICAL COLORS — Colors used throughout the church calendar year, purple or blue, green, white, red and black.

NARTHEX — The vestibule or area between the front door and the nave.

NAVE — The large area of the church where the congregation is seated, extending from the chancel to the back.

OFFICE LIGHTS — All candles on the retable, usually in groups of three, five or seven.

PASCHAL CANDLE — A very large candle, often set in an ornate candlestick, usually placed in the chancel on Holy Saturday and lighted for each service thereafter until Ascension Day.

PULPIT — A rostrum, frequently elevated, from which the sermon is preached.

REREDOS — A carved or painted panel of wood or stone on the wall behind the altar.

RETABLE — A shelf at the base of the reredos for placing the altar cross, flowers and office lights.

ROOD SCREEN — A partition of iron grillwork or carved wood separating the nave from the chancel.

SANCTUARY — The holiest area of the church in which the altar stands.

TABERNACLE — A carved box-like receptacle for the consecrated elements, often fixed to the middle of the altar.

TRACT RACK — a compartmental device holding leaflets, booklets and other printed matter.

VESICA — An aureole or pointed oval shape surrounding a sacred image.